ACCLAIM FOR M.... STUFF

"Josh is a good friend of mine and a great example of what a Christian husband, father, and man should be. This book is a good guide for anyone looking to improve in any area of their life."

— Rich Froning, Three-time
CrossFit Games Champion

"Josh Turner is the real deal. On top of being a talented song-writer and touring artist, he's a strong Christian and devoted family man. I've been in the woods duck hunting with Josh, at the beach with his family, and backstage with him. He is the same authentic and consistent gentleman wherever he is. This book offers spiritual insight to men, encouraging us to be better husbands, dads, and men of God. Josh shares stories that will make you laugh and inspire you with lessons in integrity that will change the way you think about what it means to be a man."

— Mike Huckabee, former
Arkansas Governor, former Host
of the HUCKABEE Television
Show, Fox News Channel
and The Huckabee Report,
Nationally syndicated daily
radio commentary

MAN STUFF

★ ★ ★ ★ ★

Devotional Thoughts on Faith, Family, and Fatherhood

JOSH TURNER

An Imprint of Thomas Nelson Publishers

THOMAS NELSON
Since 1798

Published in Nashville, Tennessee, by Thomas Nelson. Thomas Nelson is a registered trademark of HarperCollins Christian Publishing, Inc.

Josh Turner representation: Modern Management, Inc.

Thank you to John Blase for his assistance with the manuscript.

Thomas Nelson titles may be purchased in bulk for educational, business, fund-raising, or sales promotional use. For information, please e-mail SpecialMarkets@ThomasNelson.com.

ISBN 978-1-4002-4089-0 (audiobook)
ISBN 978-0-7180-1143-7 (eBook)
ISBN 978-1-4002-4557-4 (TP)

This book is dedicated to:

my wife, Jennifer;

my sons, Hampton, Colby, and Marion;

my parents, Joe and Karen;

my siblings, Carrie and Matt;

my grandparents,
Drexell and Dora Turner; F. E. and Carolyn Weaver;

and my in-laws, Joe and Charlotte.

To my heroes, my friends, and my fans:

thank you for the love, support, discipline,

and encouragement that have made me

the man that I am.

CONTENTS

FOREWORD

was introduced to Josh Turner one winter day while driving the back roads of my family's hunting property. My radio was blaring when the song "Long Black Train" by Josh came on. I immediately fell in love with the tune, and Josh's deep bass voice was impressive. However, I was surprised and delighted to

Jase Robertson and me, West Monroe, LA

discover the lyrics of the song had a spiritual connotation and dealt with overcoming various forms of temptation. Anyone who knows me understands that I am not ashamed to declare that Jesus Christ is Lord of my life. I believe God uses human beings, despite our flaws, to spread the good news of Jesus to this world we live in. The good news that Jesus Christ became God in flesh, died on a cross for our mistakes, and rose from the dead to give us hope of living forever gives meaning and purpose to our lives. I surrendered to Christ when I was fourteen years old and was privileged to be baptized by my father in the river that ran in front of our house. Jesus Christ produced a relationship with God in my life and brought my family together in a special way. My work as a duck call builder and my role on the TV show, *Duck Dynasty*, is my platform for making the gospel of Christ known.

I felt a common connection with Josh as I followed his singing career because he seemed to be using his talents as a platform for God, much like I do. I met Josh for the first time in person at a charity event put on by a mutual friend. Josh and I formed a friendship that night and, even though I was a bit disappointed with his lack of facial hair, I was impressed with his heart for God. I figured any man with that kind of booming voice should be a pass for frequently shaving. Even though I am joking about having a beard, I do think this world needs men that are proud to be men and should assume spiritual leadership roles in our society and homes. My dad once told me that an endangered species on our planet was men who are the spiritual leaders of their family and are not ashamed to declare Jesus as Lord.

Josh and I have a common goal to go to heaven, and we understand that our top priority is to get our family there as well. Through our growing friendship, Josh was nice enough to join my family in the making of our Christmas album, *Duck the Halls, A Robertson Family Christmas*. Josh wrote the song "Why I Love Christmas" and performed it as a duet with my wife Missy. My favorite line of the song is "the Child that was born on that mornin' brought the gift of salvation to us". That line sums up the power of Christ in our lives by offering mankind forgiveness and a relationship with an eternal God. The night the Christmas album was released, Josh and his family came to my house for a celebration in hope that God could use us all to promote Christ through our album. We laughed, shared and prayed together as members of God's forever family often do.

I am honored that Josh asked me to be a part of this book because the principles of faith, family and fatherhood are qualities that bring joy to our homes, communities, and ultimately heaven. I am proud to call Josh my friend and brother, and this book inspires me to be a spiritual leader through Christ. Josh shares from his heart and experiences and is sincerely honest about how God uses us in our strengths, despite our weaknesses. If God can use Josh and me to spread the knowledge of his Son, He can use you as well. Let's do this. We will plan on seeing you in heaven if not sooner.

Jase Robertson

Colby, Jennifer, Hampton, Me, and Marion, November 2012

INTRODUCTION

I was raised in a strong Christian family in a tight-knit community in rural South Carolina. I was taught essential life lessons, like the value of a dollar, what hard work feels like, and how important an education is. I was taught why being thoughtful, respectful, and considerate of others makes life more fulfilling, and why trusting God with your life's decisions is wise. If all that sounds a little old-fashioned, well, that's because it is. And I'm okay with that.

But, frankly, I'm not okay with the fact that it's hard being a man of character, especially when men's roles have changed so much over a relatively short period of time. Things just aren't like they used to be twenty or thirty years ago. Not even five years ago! Life has become much faster and more complicated; traditional values aren't politically correct. And even with my grounded upbringing, I find myself wishing it were easier to be the man I want to be in my roles as husband, father, son, friend, but it's not. Yet the challenges that go with the territory make me look to God all the more. And that's a good thing!

As I've grown over the years, God has taught me a lot. So

it's my hope that the stories I share in these pages encourage you—that they will instill courage *in* you—for those times when your roles and responsibilities feel too heavy to carry or just plain hard to fulfill. The image of the strong, self-sufficient man doing life easily on his own is just that: an image, an illusion. We men need one another if we are to be the men God wants us to be.

In this book you'll learn a little bit more about how God has shaped and continues to shape me. You'll also learn about my wife, my boys, and the family I grew up in. I hope you see that the everyday small things in this life really do add up to matter a great deal in the long run. And I hope you'll smile—even laugh—and gain a little wisdom along the way. Maybe even a lot.

A MAN AT PEACE

A heart at peace gives life to the body,
but envy rots the bones.

PROVERBS 14:30 NIV

ntegrity. The word means "things fit together" or "things are as they should be." And when things are as they should be, I can be at peace. That's one reason why I want to be like that, a man of integrity. I want my sons to be able to look at me and say, "Daddy's a man at peace." I want to be a man of integrity, but I sometimes fall short.

Here's a question: what's the worst thing you could imagine happening on a photo shoot for Bassmaster Classic? Bingo! The fish won't bite! This happened to me recently. Not that there weren't any fish biting, but just not fish of the right size. We spent the day on the lake doing everything right, but all I could reel in were small fry. Nothing big and manly and worthy of the title "Master of the Bass"! We were burning daylight, so my guide finally said, "Josh, I caught a big one earlier today. Wanna use it?"

And there I was, faced with one of those moments when I had to choose what kind of a man I was going to be. And I took the bait. I said, "Yes." We got the big one out of the cooler, I struck my best pose, and he snapped the photo. Mission accomplished. "Head for the shore, fellas!"

While that may have been a great photo, it wasn't a great moment for me. To tell the truth, it was awful. I didn't act with integrity—and I knew it. The fish in that picture? It didn't "fit" the actual circumstances. Things in that picture were not as they should have been.

It may sound corny, but I felt dirty after that experience. I felt like a dog that had rolled in the muck and needed a good hosing off. It wasn't my guide's fault, and it sure wasn't that fish's fault. It was all Josh's fault. I made the decision to do something that didn't fit with who I want to be. Basically, I blew it. I haven't been all the way around the block, but I've been far enough around to know you only get so many chances to blow it in this life before the people closest to you—the people you love and care about the most, like your sons and your wife—start to doubt you. Oh, they'll keep on loving you, but they're just not sure they can always trust you.

I don't want to be that kind of father or husband or friend or man. I want to be a man of integrity—so that my heart will be a place at peace, peaceful like the glass-smooth surface of a bass-filled lake at dusk.

Sometimes choosing the little fish makes you the bigger man.

DON'T LET IT GET THE BEST OF YOU

The Lord is my helper; I will not be afraid.

HEBREWS 13:6

When it comes to fears, I've got a few. The first that comes to mind is deep, dark water. To me, being in an abyss is the epitome of feeling helpless and overwhelmed.

On our one-year anniversary Jennifer and I went to Jamaica. That was when I first gave snorkeling a try, but I didn't last very long. When I first stuck my head down in the water and saw the coral reef right in front of me, I was fine. But when, in my peripheral vision, I caught sight of the depth and darkness of the ocean, I literally started hyperventilating, something I'd never experienced before. I guess the best way to describe it is, I freaked out! I grew up about an hour from the ocean, and I've seen a lot of crazy things in and around the water. Plus, as I've gotten older, I've learned about rip currents and sharks and stingrays and other sea creatures, so I have a healthy respect for it all.

The other fear I'd mention is a much more personal one: it's being gone from Jennifer and my boys. When I say gone, I mean separated from them . . . permanently. Just the thought of that gives me a heartbreaking, hurt feeling. I actually wrote a song recently about the possibility of being apart. It's called "Being Gone from You," and it's probably the only song I've ever written that makes me shed tears and get choked up when I'm singing it. It's just a very personal, emotionally deep song that talks about my greatest personal fear.

But I've learned from experience that, if you're not careful, fear will get the best of you, maybe even the *very* best of you. Fear can keep you from people and experiences that could enhance your life. For example, I've seen cases in my own family where parents are so fearful for their children— so scared they're going to get hurt or sick—that they really shelter them, if not smother them. Then their children miss chances for going out into the world and making their own mistakes. Unfortunately, instead of drawing the child closer, all it does in the end is push the child away.

I believe it's best to deal with fear in the opposite way. If you look in the Bible, you'll see that "fear not" is one of the most consistent messages you'll find. I lean on the verse that says, "Do not be anxious about anything" (Philippians 4:6 NIV). So that's what I do: I pray and give the fear to God and trust Him to give me courage. Now don't get me wrong. It's okay to be scared. Being scared is a natural emotion and a good reaction to some things. And in certain situations the feeling of fear can literally save your life! But feeling fear and living in fear are two very different things. And God clearly doesn't want us to live in fear.

When Jennifer and I celebrated our ten-year anniversary, we went to Hawaii. With her encouragement I decided to give snorkeling another try. I managed to get in the water, figure out how to breathe through the snorkel, swim down into the water, and actually have a great time. I really did. I believe that, with God's help, I overcame my fear of deep water enough to try snorkeling again. I even got to see a green sea turtle—something I would've missed if I'd let fear have the best of me.

FEELING FEAR AND LIVING IN FEAR ARE TWO VERY DIFFERENT THINGS. AND GOD CLEARLY DOESN'T WANT US TO LIVE IN FEAR.

DREAMS REQUIRE HARD WORK AND REST

"Be still, and know that I am God."

PSALM 46:10 NIV

I knew at an early age I had a talent for singing. My parents did too; they could see it. When I turned thirteen, it became a dream of mine to take my talent somewhere, so I started singing at ball games and beauty pageants, basically anywhere anybody would let me sing. By the time I was seventeen, which was the summer of '95, I was playing guitar and writing my own songs. Between then and the summer of '96, I started working at a local farm supply warehouse. I realized this warehouse was full of a lot of dust, chemicals, and pesticides. But what I didn't realize was, I was ruining my voice by breathing in all that junk and by *not* knowing how to sing properly or take care of my voice.

I'll never forget the day I started singing along to a Tim McGraw song and felt physical pain. I knew right then something was wrong. I told Mama, "My voice hurts. It hurts to sing." She took me to a local doctor, and he advised us to go to the Vanderbilt Voice Clinic. What they found was a lesion on my right vocal cord. Fortunately they said, "The Lord does better healing than we do, so we're not going to do any kind of procedure." I was put on vocal rest for a year. I was also told to drink plenty of water and to stay away from alcohol and caffeine—and from that chemical-laden warehouse!

Another part of my rehab was working with vocal coach Sharyn Mapes in Florence, South Carolina. I'd visit her once a week after school and sing classical vocal music (also part of the doctors' approach to my healing). That was an extremely hard season for me because I couldn't do what I loved to do—sing country music. (I did learn to whistle real good though!) At the end of that year, I started easing back into singing country, but I used the classical techniques I had learned.

In August 1998, I transferred to Belmont University in Nashville, right back into the world of classical music and theory. I knew I was still struggling. The truth is, I was fatigued from such a taxing experience. But the pain gradually started going away, my endurance returned, and I started noticing my range had gotten a lot bigger and the texture of my voice was like never before. What I initially thought was a big problem turned out to be a huge blessing in disguise.

I'll never forget sitting down at Belmont one day, singing a Randy Travis song called "The Hole," and hearing

Me giving Carrie and Matt a music lesson

myself thinking, *Wow, now this is really special! Only God could've seen how all this would work out.*

The days and weeks and months of rest had paid off, and my voice not only healed but became stronger. Plus, I then knew all about my vocal cords and what I would need to do to care for them over the course of the career I dreamed of.

Actually, the truth is, God healed me. I just had to be still for a while and let Him.

PLAY BY THE RULES

No one serving as a soldier gets entangled in the concerns
of civilian life; he seeks to please the recruiter. Also,
if anyone competes as an athlete, he is not crowned
unless he competes according to the rules.

2 TIMOTHY 2:4–5

In the early days of my career, we all traveled on the same bus. By *we all* I mean my wife, Jennifer, the crew, the band, everybody. That's just how it is when you're starting out. But I felt convicted that we needed some rules, some bus rules. So I posted a list in the bus. There were actually quite a few, but here are four I remember:

1. No women on the bus unless they're family.
2. No alcohol, drugs, or smoking.
3. Clean up after yourself.
4. We play country music and we dress the part.

I remember playing at the Grand Ole Opry several years ago, and a member of another band got on our bus and "took" the rules and hung them up in the men's bathroom of the Opry. As you might guess, this got me and my list a lot of attention—negative attention. *Billboard* magazine even included it in a story they were doing at the time on touring in the music industry. My reaction to the whole thing was "What's the big deal? I'm not ashamed of the rules on my bus. I don't care what anybody else thinks about it. It's *my* bus."

I don't post my bus rules anymore. Everybody who works for me knows what I expect, and they abide by those expectations—or they don't work for me. I believe this is the way it is with our heavenly Father. God has rules and expects us to abide by them. This is His world, and He knows how it works best. If we don't want to follow His rules, we're free to find another bus. But His is the only one that'll get us to where we really need to be.

IF WE DON'T WANT TO FOLLOW [GOD'S] RULES, WE'RE FREE TO FIND ANOTHER BUS. BUT HIS IS THE ONLY ONE THAT'LL GET US TO WHERE WE REALLY NEED TO BE.

MAKING A LIST

Don't worry about anything, but in everything,
through prayer and petition with thanksgiving,
let your requests be made known to God.

PHILIPPIANS 4:6

You know those stories about how God answered prayer right down to the tiniest of details? Well, Jennifer and I have a story like that, and it involves our home.

In 2004 we were living in a brick home patterned after an old farmhouse. It was very well built and we loved it, but it was right in the middle of a neighborhood with a shared gravel drive, and we soon found ourselves craving some privacy and space.

So in late 2007 we started seriously looking for a new house with some land. We looked and looked all over the Nashville area but just couldn't find exactly what we wanted. Our realtor was helping us too. All of us were constantly on the Internet looking at listings trying to find *our* place. Well, Jennifer and I got home from church one Sunday, and we started looking at listings. That's when she said, "I think we need to make a list of everything we want in a home and property, and then pray over it." I thought that was a great idea, so we did: we made our list and prayed over it.

Almost immediately we felt the Lord telling us to look for land instead of a house. Prior to that we were opposed to building; we just didn't think we had the time to get involved in all that building would mean. The idea was just overwhelming. But we really felt God leading us that way. We talked it over with our business manager and with our realtor. The two of them said they felt good about it too, so we changed our focus and started looking for land. Again, we looked and looked, but there was always something just not quite right with every property we looked at.

Then one day our realtor sent us a "land" listing just a few miles from where we were living at the time, but it already had a house on it. It was a brand-new listing—it hadn't even been on the market twenty-four hours—so we made an appointment to see it. We were the first prospective buyers, and as we drove onto the property, it was almost like walking through the pearly gates. This property had everything on our list. Everything! It was amazing. There were old barns on it from the 1800s, a creek ran through the property, it was close to forty acres, the house was well built, it had a shop, the grounds offered plenty of space for our boys to run and play—I could go on and on.

To this day we have no idea why the property was listed under the land MLS since it had a house on it, but that's the way it was! We also realized that, had we not prayed about it and started looking for land like the Lord told us to, we never would have found it. So it was very obvious that God was taking care of us and testing us at the same time.

I'm grateful that Jennifer suggested making a list and then praying over it. That invited God into our decision-making process. It wasn't that He wasn't in it to begin with, but it was a very tangible way of saying, "We want a change, but we want to be led by You, Lord." God answered our prayer, every detail and then some.

A MAN NEEDS FRIENDS

Iron sharpens iron,
and one man sharpens another.

PROVERBS 27:17

I was somewhat of a loner growing up. I did have a best friend or two as I got older, but one of those went down a different path than me. Other friends would get close but then move away or do something I didn't agree with, so I'd part ways. I didn't place a huge value on fighting for friendships. If you hurt me, you might get another chance, but maybe not. I was fine and dandy by myself.

But one day I asked myself, *If my wife and children were taken from me, who would I have? Who could I depend on outside of my family?* The answers scared me. So that night I committed to nurturing my friendships, especially my friendships with men, and doing a better job at being a good friend.

A man needs friends. He needs other men who will hold him accountable, encourage him, and lend a listening ear. And sometimes a man just needs another man to sit together and laugh with. Yes, it's that important. Many times I get set in my ways, and I'm intimidated by being asked to step out of my comfort zone. I'm convinced this has kept me from fostering male friends throughout my life.

Early in the book of Genesis, God told Adam that it is not good for man to be alone. What we've learned since then is, it's also not good for man to be a loner.

GOD TOLD ADAM
THAT IT IS NOT
GOOD FOR MAN TO
BE ALONE. WHAT
WE'VE LEARNED
SINCE THEN IS,
IT'S ALSO NOT
GOOD FOR MAN
TO BE A LONER.

COUNT ON IT

Now above all, my brothers, do not swear,
either by heaven or by earth or with any other oath.
Your "yes" must be "yes," and your "no" must be
"no," so that you won't fall under judgment.

JAMES 5:12

If Daddy said he was going to do something, you could believe it would happen.

One time my brother and I were walking down the dirt road beside our house with Daddy, and he said, "You see that power line? I can hit it with a rock on the first try." Then he picked up a rock and hit the line!

One of the craziest things I've seen concerning Daddy's credibility happened in the drive-through lane at Hardee's. We were sitting in line after placing our order, and Daddy said, "I bet I can spit my gum in that trash can over there." Even though Daddy was competent in situations like this, the trash can wasn't close by. But he leaned back and spit his gum, and it landed on the lower edge of the can's lid. And then Daddy's gum rolled up the lid and into the opening! We simply could not believe it!

I don't know if we were impressed so much with what Daddy did as we were with who Daddy was: he was and is a man who will do what he says he will do. Trust me!

BELIEVING IN MYSELF

We will no longer be little children, tossed by the waves and
blown around by every wind of teaching, by human cunning with
cleverness in the techniques of deceit. But speaking the truth in
love, let us grow in every way into Him who is the head—Christ.

EPHESIANS 4:14-15

A lot of my success has come from just believing in myself and
in the talents God has given me, no matter what anybody
around me is saying. I've learned you'll always have *en*couragers and *dis*couragers. When you're chasing a dream, you have
to learn to sift through what people are telling you and saying
about you.

From my early teenage years, through high school and
into college, I had the dream of being a country music singer
and getting a record deal. That was all I talked about. You
could see my dream in the way I dressed and acted. Even my
bedroom when I was in high school was decorated in a country theme, complete with pictures of country artists all over
the walls, a couch covered in cowhide print fabric, and a coffee table made out of an old wagon wheel. It was a dream I was

really trying to achieve, so I surrounded myself with what I loved and symbols of what I wanted for my life.

But there were a lot of naysayers. Here are a couple of funny naysayer stories. The first involves a girl in my high school Spanish class. We were seniors, we had known each other for years, and we always picked at each other in a sort of love-hate relationship, so to speak. She started singing songs in Spanish class. I don't really remember why, but she did. I started joking with her and making fun of her. Well, one particular day when she was singing and I was making fun of her, she turned around and let me have it, saying something to the effect of "You'll never be as good as Reba McEntire!" Five years later I ended up getting a record deal with MCA—the same label that signed Reba McEntire.

The other story shows my commitment to my dream of becoming a country music star. During our high school graduation, I really felt convicted about wearing a cowboy hat to symbolize how serious I was about my goals and where I wanted to be one day. Plus, I never was a fan of mortarboards; they just seemed to cramp my style and individualism. I really wanted to make a statement to all those people I went to school with who didn't believe in me and said I couldn't catch my dream. So I did: I wore a cowboy hat—complete with tassel hanging down the side—to my high school graduation.

Graduation day, Hannah-Pamplico High School

Some people loved it. Some people hated it. But I really didn't care. It was my last high school moment, and I had bigger fish to fry.

There's a line between believing in yourself and believing you're better than everyone else. Cross that line and you end up prideful, and pride comes before a great fall. But staying on the healthy side of that line shows that you believe with all your heart in the dreams God has for you. And if you believe you're supposed to wear a cowboy hat to graduation, just know you're not the first!

THERE'S A LINE BETWEEN BELIEVING IN YOURSELF AND BELIEVING YOU'RE BETTER THAN EVERYONE ELSE.

ADVICE FROM EDDY

Listen to counsel and receive instruction
so that you may be wise later in life.

PROVERBS 19:20

When I was a student at Belmont University in Nashville, I was a regular at this little restaurant off 8th Avenue called Melpark Restaurant. Quite a few celebrities and country music stars would frequent there. One of these was Eddy Arnold, a country singer who had songs on the charts for seven decades and who sold over 90 million records. One day I went up and introduced myself, and I found him to be one of the most down-to-earth, genuine men I'd ever met. He was not arrogant at all, and it seemed the more often I ran into him, the nicer he got.

Eddy and I ended up hanging out every so often. There were times I'd actually sit down and eat with him, and he'd pay for my meal. He gave me a lot of great advice during those meals, advice like "Be wise with your money" and "Always record love songs." One piece of advice really struck me as odd: "If you find a song that's right for Josh Turner, record it even if your enemy wrote it." At the time Eddy's words didn't mean that much to me and, quite honestly, I didn't really understand what he meant. But several years later I found out.

I was working on another album, and there was a particular song I really struggled with because I didn't see eye to eye with one of the writers. Then Eddy's words came to mind and I realized what he was basically trying to say to me: "Don't hold a grudge and don't harbor bitterness, especially when it comes to a song that might be a hit or even be a career song." So I took his advice, and I'm glad I did because the song was a success.

I don't believe I came by Eddy Arnold's advice by accident or coincidence. Especially since I received it a little ahead of the time I would need to apply it. The way I see it, God gave me just what I needed at just the right time for making a good and wise decision. And how cool of God to give me that advice by way of Eddy Arnold!

MAMA'S IDEA

The one who has contempt for instruction will pay the penalty,
but the one who respects a command will be rewarded.

PROVERBS 13:13

Author John Eldredge writes, "Masculinity is bestowed. A boy learns who he is and what he's got from a man, or the company of men." There's not a doubt in my mind this is a true statement, and masculinity is usually bestowed by way of the father. But it's also just as true that you can learn a lot of things from your mama. A lot of good things.

I wouldn't trade my mama for the world. She sacrificed so much of her time taking me to all those auditions. She was essentially my "car service" during those very early years. She was also the rock I leaned on when I had terrible stage fright. Mama grew up singing and playing the piano and guitar. She knew those gifts were in my blood too, but that it was my dream to take them further than she had. So she pushed me to do things I never would have done on my own, and her love has gotten me to where I am today.

I went on my first date in the tenth grade. This girl lived

thirty minutes from where I lived. I had just learned to drive, not to mention I didn't know how a date was supposed to go. Before I left, Mama walked me out on the front porch and around to her rose garden. Then she let me cut the rose of my choice. That was something itself, but then she said, "Cut one more rose." I asked Mama who the second rose was for. She said, "That's for *her* mama."

I was crazy about that girl, and after those moments on the front porch, I knew my mama was on my side. After presenting that second rose, I knew my girlfriend's mama was too. Showing respect will carry you a long way in this life. I owe that idea to my mama, among many other good things.

SHOWING RESPECT WILL CARRY YOU A LONG WAY IN THIS LIFE.

COMMUNITY

You were called to be free, brothers; only don't use this
freedom as an opportunity for the flesh, but serve one
another through love. For the entire law is fulfilled in
one statement: Love your neighbor as yourself.

GALATIANS 5:13–14

'll never forget September 1989. That was when Hurricane
Hugo hit the Atlantic coastline. Hannah, South Carolina, is
about an hour inland. I'll always remember my family hud-
dling together in my parents' bedroom all night long as that
storm came through. We said a prayer as a family, asking
God to protect us and our home. It was a long night, and we
couldn't sleep until the storm died down. It was one of the
scariest experiences of my life.

When we got up the next morning, we were surprised to
find fifty-something trees down in our yard—and that only
one shingle had been blown off the house! That's right. One
shingle! It still gives me chills just thinking about how all
those trees fell away from the house instead of on it.

We went without power for two weeks, took baths in

Lynches River, and ate supper by candlelight. Daddy had to buy a generator to keep our refrigerator and freezer running. There was even a relief unit from Arkansas that came to feed us two meals a day. It was also the only time I remember going to church and nobody was dressed up. We gathered as a church body to pray for restoration and healing. As bad as that time was, it was also good. The community came together and shared what they had. It was a time of lending your neighbors a hand and a heart. It was a picture of what community really means.

A STEWARD OF THE LAND

God blessed [the man and the woman], and God
said to them, "Be fruitful, multiply, fill the earth, and
subdue it. Rule the fish of the sea, the birds of the sky,
and every creature that crawls on the earth."

GENESIS 1:28

I've always loved deer hunting. I learned the ways of hunting as a boy. I was taught about guns and safety and camouflage and deer stands and everything else involved with the sport. But let's face it: I hunted for sport. I was young then and full of trigger-itch. I hadn't yet learned to be a steward of the land.

Being a steward of the land involves seeing what things really mean and how they fit together in God's grand scheme. It involves realizing that there's so much

Quail hunting, Pamplico, SC

One of three 8-point bucks I took in one week in September 2008, Hannah, SC

more to hunting than trophies on a wall.

As I've gotten older, I've learned that killing a deer provides meat for my family. Providing for them in this way gives me a great deal of satisfaction, much more than being able to brag about the score of the buck's antlers. After I've killed a deer, I say a prayer of thanksgiving to the Lord for that animal. Another one of God's creatures gave its life to provide for me and mine.

I guess what I'm saying is that, for me, the meaning of hunting has changed. I've put away the boyish delight in the kill and replaced it with a man's attitude toward caring for those lives entrusted to him, and that includes the animal in the crosshairs. That's thinking about tomorrow as well as today. That's being a steward of the land.

THE LEAST OF THESE

"The King will answer them, 'I assure you: Whatever you did for one
of the least of these brothers of Mine, you did for Me.'"

JESUS IN MATTHEW 25:40

When I was about twelve years old, we had a huge garden behind our house. One hot summer day my family and I were working in that garden. Our house sat right on Highway 378 in Hannah, South Carolina, and that highway was always full of beach traffic in the summer. While we were in the garden, this car came flying down the dirt road beside our house. The driver slowed down, did a little three-point turn, and backed into our property. Then he got out of the driver's side, jerked his little girl out of the backseat, and started beating her. My daddy took off running toward them.

Apparently the little girl had gotten sick and thrown up in the car, and her daddy lost it. My daddy got up in that guy's face and said, "Don't you ever lay a hand on that girl like that again. Get in the car and get outta here!" The man got in the car and got outta there just like my daddy told him to. Daddy and I went right back to working in the garden.

It would have been easy for my daddy to have stood there and watch the whole thing, thinking something like, *That's none of my business.* But he didn't do the easy thing; it *was* his business. When you think about it, standing up for a child, for someone weaker, is *always* our business. It's always hard, but in that moment my daddy was not just standing up for that little girl; he was standing up for Jesus.

That was the first time I'd seen my daddy act that way— so quick and dramatic. It made a lasting impact on me and taught me that, while some things aren't any of our business, some things, like standing up for innocent children, definitely are.

STANDING UP FOR
A CHILD, FOR
SOMEONE WEAKER,
IS *ALWAYS* OUR
BUSINESS.

THE THRILL AND THE AGONY

Don't you know that the runners in a stadium all race, but only one
receives the prize? Run in such a way to win the prize.

1 CORINTHIANS 9:24

These days there are sports leagues with no winners, no los-
ers, no outs, and no strikes. And I think it's completely
ridiculous. It's important for children to know the range of
human emotions that come with winning and losing; they
need to know what winning and losing feel like. What do
these emotions prepare them for? My answer is, "real life in
the real world."

There are gonna be rough seasons in a child's life—times
when things don't go as expected and things don't get handed
to him. In those times it's important to be a good loser and
accept the way things are. And when the good times roll
around, it's important to learn to be a good winner, to be
pleased and proud of one's accomplishments, but not arrogant (and there's a difference).

Competitive sports provide a safe place for learning
invaluable life lessons such as self-discipline, taking care of

your physical body, time management, and not taking the game too seriously. You also learn about being a part of a team. This is just the beginning of a long list of things you can learn when there's one clear winner and one clear loser.

I realize many folks would disagree with me. But I believe it's important to run with purpose, in such a way as to get the prize. And who doesn't want the prize?!

WHAT'S RIGHT AND SMART

Children, obey your parents as you would
the Lord, because this is right.

EPHESIANS 6:1

While I was growing up, I obeyed my parents . . . most of the time. But there were a few times I didn't. I call them my backfiring moments, and two of them are quite memorable.

One time my brother and I decided to take one of his friends out on Lynches River. His friend had never really experienced a blackwater river, and we thought he needed to. So we got Daddy's jonboat all ready, put it in the water, and off we went. The only thing Daddy said to us before we left was "Whatever you do, don't go downstream."

Being the oldest of three, I'd had a lot of experience on the river with Daddy. We'd been on that river together probably a thousand times, and nine out of every ten we went upstream. I knew upstream; I knew what it looked like and felt like; I knew what to expect. But that day downstream held some allure, and I let my temptation get the best of me. I reasoned that it would be exciting and adventurous. Besides, my brother and his friend were with me, and they'd be able to help out if we got into any trouble.

Well, we started flying downstream, and it wasn't ten minutes into our ride when all of a sudden we hit a log. The impact flipped the motor up and out of the water, then back down, killing it. We tried—we really tried—but we couldn't get it to crank back up. We had paddles, but the boat was too big and heavy for us to be able to paddle upstream. And we didn't have a trolling motor, so there we were, stranded, just drifting in the river, headed farther downstream.

We'd gotten on the river about an hour before dark, so the sun was setting quickly, and nothing ahead of us was familiar to me. As we drifted, the water level became shallower; the shoreline, narrower, and the conditions, more treacherous. We ended up drifting through a lot of trees, which are very tricky to maneuver through in the daylight, not to mention the *dark*!

At that point I decided I needed to swallow my pride and call my daddy on my cell phone. I told him what had happened and asked him where he could meet us. He came—eventually—and picked us up at a landing, but it was hours after dark by the time he found us. It was a very humbling moment for me. Daddy was not happy, and my brother's friend was scared out of his mind. Needless to say, I avoided downstream from then on!

Another backfire moment happened on a ski trip I went on with my high school buddies. I had never skied before. Daddy had been a few times, so I borrowed his suit and gear. When I asked him if there was anything I needed to know, he said, "If you get to goin' too fast, just fall on your butt."

On Lynches River . . . upstream, of course!

So off we headed to the mountains, and I got started on the bunny slope. Having done pretty well, I was thinking, *Man, I've got this.* So my friend and I took the lift up to the highest slope. From the lift I saw some skiers bend their knees and tuck down, so I figured I'd give that a try. And when I did, I quickly found myself flying down the mountain. I looked at the people down at the bottom of the slope and had that feeling of *I'm either goin' to kill somebody or myself!*

What I should have done was fall on my butt like Daddy told me. But I decided to fall to one side, sorta like sliding into second base—a move, I discovered, that works in baseball but not in downhill skiing. I started tumbling, felt something in my shoulder pop, landed on my back, and finally slid to a stop. I opened my eyes and looked straight up into the sky. Another skier came over to where I was laying and said, "Man, I've never seen anybody go that fast down this slope! You must have been going 65–70 mph!" The paramedics came, took me to the emergency room, and, after some tests, told me I'd torn my rotator cuff. I haven't been snow skiing since, but if I decide to go again, I know how *not* to fall.

Obeying your parents is right. It's also smart.

LISTEN CLOSE

Then [God] said, "Go out and stand on the
mountain in the Lord's presence."
At that moment, the Lord passed by. A great and mighty wind was
tearing at the mountains and was shattering cliffs before
the Lord, but the Lord was not in the wind. After the wind there
was an earthquake, but the Lord was not in the earthquake.
After the earthquake there was a fire, but the Lord was not in
the fire. And after the fire there was a voice, a soft whisper.

1 KINGS 19:11–12

graduated from high school in May of 1996. At that same
time my daddy received a promotion from Farm Bureau
Insurance Company that involved my parents and siblings
moving an hour away to the coast of South Carolina. I stayed
behind, living in the house where I'd grown up, and started
college at Francis Marion University. It was a good experience, but I admit it was a little weird.

All through my teenage years, I'd been praying about
getting a record deal and running the scenarios through my
mind of how all that might happen. One day, at the house by

myself, I got on my four-wheeler and rode around the fields behind the house praying, asking God some hard questions about country music as a career. I asked honestly, "God, is this even possible? Can I make it to Nashville?"

I kept riding and finally got quiet enough to hear His still, small voice. It was almost a whisper: "Josh, if this is what you want, I'll give it to you on one condition: you have to trust Me no matter what. I'm going to create My own path for you, different from anybody else's."

Here I am, twelve years into this career of mine, and I'm still trusting Him. I still have days when doubts are thick, but thinking about that moment from years ago and what He's done since always puts those fears to rest. I didn't want to be a flash in the pan; I wanted to be a legend in country music. No matter how rough things have been or will be, I learned a long time ago the power of listening to God's whisper. When God makes a promise, He always keeps it.

FISH AND SNAKES

"Now go; I'm sending you out like lambs among wolves."

JESUS IN LUKE 10:3

Colby and I went fishing with my daddy the other day on Lynches River. It was a lot of fun. The weather was perfect, and the water level was good for fishing. It was just a beautiful day. We threw our lines in the water and actually got some bites, which is not always the case these days. For the past five to ten years, the fishing hasn't been that great. You used to be able to catch the limit every time. But it's not that way anymore. I don't have any research to back this, but my personal opinion is that the overabundance of gar—which feed on the other game fish—has caused the game fish numbers to decline. That's just what I think. But even so, it's still a joy to be on the river with Colby and Daddy, fishing for bream. Daddy and I both caught some that were nice sized.

Colby and I had a scare, though. We almost drifted right onto a water moccasin—and it scared me half to death. I didn't see it until we were right up on it! That snake was perfectly camouflaged—and it was actually the second snake we'd seen that day, so I felt pretty unnerved. I was telling Daddy about it, and he said, "It seems like I spend most of my time lookin' for snakes instead of fishin'." He also told me what Papa Turner used to say: "The more snakes you see on the river, the better the fishin'."

Papa Turner's statement got me to thinking. That's sorta the way it is in life. In order to get the things you need or want—be it catching a fish or getting a job or fulfilling a dream—you have to be willing to go out there and face the snakes. You need to face those people or situations that you may not be comfortable with or that may really scare you. Staying in your little comfort zone, wherever that is, means you'll never be free to conquer the challenges that can potentially enrich your life and the life of your family. You have to be willing to face the snakes if you want to catch the fish. That's the way it is on the river, and that's the way it is in life.

IN ORDER TO GET
THE THINGS YOU
NEED OR WANT—BE
IT CATCHING A FISH
OR GETTING A JOB
OR FULFILLING A
DREAM—YOU HAVE
TO BE WILLING TO
GO OUT THERE AND
FACE THE SNAKES.

HARD WORDS

"Much will be required of everyone who has been
given much. And even more will be expected of the
one who has been entrusted with more."

JESUS IN LUKE 12:48

During my first semester of college, I was living in my family's house all by myself. My parents had moved when Daddy got a new job in another county. Did I mention I was living in our house all by myself?

At the time I didn't want to be going to college. I wasn't interested in it at all. The only thing I wanted to do was go to Nashville and sing country music. So I did the absolute minimum at school and filled the rest of my time with playing pool, fooling around with girls, and taking naps. As a result, I earned a first semester GPA of 1.7.

Daddy and Mama were at the house one day and saw the letter in the mail that reflected my grades. Daddy called me back to their bedroom and asked me to come in and shut the door. The three of us were the only ones in the house—and he told me to shut the door!! Daddy then proceeded to give me the speech of my life: "If this is the way you're gonna be, you can make your own way."

As hard as I imagine those words were to say, they were really hard to hear. Good, but hard. I went back to my room and tried to come up with some scheme for making my own way, but just came up empty. I knew what I had to do. I went and asked for forgiveness for being so slack. Daddy forgave me and then said more hard words: "If this happens again, you're out of my house."

The scheme I finally came up with was straight up the middle: go to class, buckle down and study, and raise my GPA. And I did. I raised my grades not just because I wanted to stay in the house, but because I wanted to continue to be the kind of son my parents had worked so hard to raise.

A SENSE OF HUMOR

Our mouths were filled with laughter,
our tongues with songs of joy.

PSALM 126:2 NIV

I've inherited quite a lot from my daddy's family. What I consider to be the greatest thing they've passed along to me besides my faith is the gift of laughter. My relatives on Daddy's side of the family are all positive, upbeat, funny—always finding something to laugh at.

As best I can tell, it all started with Daddy's parents. They were always clowning around, being goofy, and making fun of each other. But that's a real gift, being able to be poked fun at and laugh rather than take offense. Daddy's parents had that gift, and it was hilarious. That gift carried over into my family. Whenever my brother and my daddy and I get together, it's always fun—always.

What I've come to see is that laughter kept my daddy's family sane. It really did. They didn't have an easy life; they were poor and scrapped for everything they had. Not everything in this life makes sense. But a sense of humor helps take the edge off. Not everyone seems to have that kind of sense, though. Good old-fashioned laughter seems to be a rare gift.

I do believe the family that prays together stays together. I also know for a fact the family that laughs together stays sane in this crazy world.

Playing dress-up and being silly

NOT EVERYTHING
IN THIS LIFE
MAKES SENSE.
BUT A SENSE OF
HUMOR HELPS TAKE
THE EDGE OFF.

STAY CLOSE

A man with many friends may be harmed,
but there is a friend who stays closer than a brother.

PROVERBS 18:24

There is a friend who sticks closer than a brother—but that doesn't mean a brother can't be pretty close. That's the way it is between my brother and me. We're both very competitive and have been since we were boys. Whether it was football outside or Scrabble inside, we both wanted to win.

We've had to learn not to let competition get between us and impact our relationship. There's nothing wrong with winning until it affects you and someone else negatively, especially when that someone is family. Winning is just not worth that price.

In order to try to keep a healthy, fun perspective on the whole winning thing, my brother and I have gotten creative with our competitive moments. One memorable time we competed against each other, we decided in advance that whoever lost would have to strip down to his underwear and run around the house three times. I won't tell you who lost that day. But I will say that, in a strange way, we both won, and we've continued to win since. We've stayed close. We've stayed brothers, and I am very grateful.

WORK AND PLAY

A man will be satisfied with good
by the words of his mouth,
and the work of a man's hands will reward him.

PROVERBS 12:14

I'd like to share two things about my daddy. First, he has always provided well for his family. And his approach to providing has always looked like this: you do your work first, then play. I have a different approach. I'll work a little, play a little, then work a little, then play a little. But not Daddy. He'll work, work, work, then play.

The other thing about Daddy is that he loves to fish. He always has. But he's never had a very good boat. He's never been one to buy anything for himself unless he really needed it, and the needs of his family have always seemed greater to him.

One day Jennifer and I were headed up to my grandparents' beach house in North Carolina to spend some time with my parents. When we got there, we noticed a new boat—as in a *brand-new* boat—parked under the house (most beach houses are on stilts). When I greeted Daddy, I said, "Whose boat is this?"

He said, "Mine."

"You bought this?" I asked.

He said, "Yes."

But I could tell from his face it was hard for him to really be excited about it. I said, "This is good, right?"

He said, "I just feel guilty for spendin' that kind of money."

I put my hand on his shoulder and said, "You've done so much for us. It's about time you did somethin' for yourself. You've earned it."

My parents, Joe and Karen

That strong work ethic is a part of who Daddy is. My hope is that in these later days of his life, he can enjoy a strong play ethic as well. I believe he deserves it. He's earned it.

TREASURED

Mary was treasuring up all these things in
her heart and meditating on them.

LUKE 2:19

I grew up in a Christian household. We went to church regularly, so I was frequently exposed to church culture. But in the early days of my journey of faith, a couple things happened that were not connected formally to "church." I like to think of them, though, as seeds from which a strong oak could grow.

The first thing that happened was in the form of a gift. My daddy's parents gave me a book titled *The Book*. It was a collection of Bible stories that fascinated me. I couldn't put it down. It was in that book that I first saw a powerful and loving God. I'm forever grateful for that gift from my grandparents.

The second thing was an experience I'll never forget. I was probably nine or ten years old at the time. Living out in the country, we had to take the trash to a dumpster that was about a half mile from our house. And between our house and the dumpster were wide-open fields. One night when Daddy and I were driving to the dumpster, I noticed that it was a really clear night, but I didn't see the moon anywhere, and the stars were hard to see. We emptied out the trash, climbed back into the car, and started heading back to the house.

All of a sudden I noticed a light reflecting off the hood of the car, and I wondered what was causing it. At that moment I felt my upper body being pulled toward the windshield of the car, and I looked up in the sky. Up over the branch behind our house was a single cloud with a lighted silhouette of a Man standing with outstretched arms. I wanted so badly to tell Daddy what I was looking at, but the words just wouldn't come! I was speechless. Then I felt something pull my body back into the seat, and I watched the reflection on the hood of the car fade away. When we got home, I ran out to our barn, found a piece of paper and a pencil, and made a quick sketch of what I'd just seen so I wouldn't forget it. I kept the experience to myself for several days. I finally shared it with my parents, and they said, "Josh, if you saw it, you saw it. And we believe you."

I knew right then and there that what I'd witnessed was Jesus letting me know that He exists. There have been countless times since then when my faith was questioned or I had doubts, but I always go back to what I saw that night. It reminds me that I have no reason to doubt that I serve a living God.

These two things anchored me in God at a young age. I believed that God existed because I'd seen Him in the stories, and then I'd seen Him in the sky.

I HAVE NO REASON TO DOUBT THAT I SERVE A LIVING GOD.

PRAYER

Pray constantly.

1 THESSALONIANS 5:17

Some people think prayer has to be formal, structured, done at set times when you bow or get down on your knees. I don't think that.

For me, I've always talked to God like I'm having a conversation with someone I love. I talk with Him, laugh with Him, even cry with Him. I can do this driving down the road in the afternoon or in a crowd somewhere in the evening. Prayer isn't limited to certain places or times. There are many nights when I pray on stage, just a short prayer, asking God to give me strength and focus or whatever I need for that time.

In a very real way I'm always talking to God. That's reflected in the lyrics of my song "Me and God":

> *Ain't nobody gonna come between me and God . . .*
> *He's my Father*
> *He's my Friend*

I've had a lot of people tell me that's their favorite song. I believe that says something about us and what we hope for, even if we miss the mark sometimes. We want to be able to talk to God about anything, anytime, anywhere. And the truth is, we can. It's called prayer.

PEOPLE BREAK YOUR HEART

Cast all your anxiety on him because he cares for you.

1 PETER 5:7 NIV

The relationship I was in before I met my wife was very complex. It was the summer of 1998, and I was twenty years old. I was part of a stage show called High Stepping Country at Lakewood Campground in Myrtle Beach, South Carolina. There was a girl in the show I'd met. One night after rehearsals she asked if I wanted to take a walk on the beach. We talked awhile, and as I walked her back to her car, she kissed me. That kiss started our relationship. Not a lot of thought put into it. Just boy likes girl and vice versa.

Well, if I'm in a relationship, I'm going to be committed. That's the way I've always been—faithful like an old dog. And so that's what I was. Committed. And our relationship lasted about two and half years. During that time I ended up putting her before God in my life. I don't remember making a conscious decision to do that. It just sorta happened over time. I placed all my happiness, my hope, my everything in her.

Shortly after we started dating, I moved to Nashville, and

we began a long-distance relationship of sending letters and talking on the phone every day. I also began a time of my getting pulled into a lot of things that were not good for me, things that pulled me further and further from the Lord.

One summer day in 2000, I was back home, and this girl and I were going to spend the day together. Picnic at the beach, hang out that night—really seize the day. I called to find out when to pick her up, and she said, "I can't do this anymore. I think I'm done."

Before that moment, I hadn't really understood anything about love and relationships, about putting your everything in one person and then having that person walk away. But after that day I started to understand.

When she broke up with me, that was the start of one of the darkest times in my life. I'd always struggled with some anxiety and nervousness, but this took my anxiety to another level entirely. I quickly fell into a serious depression. The very next day I had to go back to Belmont as a single guy. I literally cried all the way from South Carolina to Nashville.

At school it was all I could do not to cry in front of people. I wrote a lot of sad, hurting songs during that time as a sort of therapy. But I started seeing a counselor on campus and slowly started to figure things out. I had put all my faith, hope, and trust in a person—someone who wasn't perfect, someone who could break my heart. The key word in that last sentence is *all*.

I went out on a few dates after that point, but none of those girls made my heart flutter. Then I met Jennifer. Meeting her wasn't planned or expected, but our friendship felt completely different. For the first time, I was truly on cloud nine. I can't really explain that time other than to say it was unbelievable.

Looking back, that dark time after the breakup was one of the best things that happened to me. It didn't feel that way at the time, but I soon learned it was. The kind of man Jennifer needed was not one who was going to put *all* of his faith, hope, and trust in her. She needed a man who put all of his faith, hope, and trust in God's hands. And since meeting her, that's what I've tried to do every day.

Jennifer and I have talked a lot about that experience. We feel blessed to have each other to lean on. I've never given myself the option of leaving Jennifer or vice versa. It took her six months to call me her boyfriend. We took it real slow, and she's mainly responsible for that. We were engaged in November of 2002 and married in June of 2003.

JESUS IS THE ANSWER

Because of the LORD's faithful love
we do not perish,
for His mercies never end.
They are new every morning;
great is Your faithfulness!

LAMENTATIONS 3:22–23

Coming out of a failed relationship in 2000 was a blessing in disguise. I was an emotional basket case. I could have easily gone the wrong way in the wake of that breakup—alcohol, sex, drugs—but I knew that was not the answer. I experienced a strange comfort in just being sad and alone. Now, being sad and alone is not the kind of thing a person goes looking for, but I've learned that when that strange peace comes, there's usually something God wants me to learn.

Up to that point in my life, I'd never been betrayed or had my heart broken. But that changed, and suddenly all those country songs I grew up on made sense. People suffer those kinds of heartbreaks every day, so if you're gonna write songs people can relate to, you've got to have the same experiences.

That painful relationship did many things to me, one of them being that I determined from that point on that my music would be real and honest.

I usually have a hard time talking about my failures. Throughout my life I've chosen to focus on the good times unless I'm writing a song about a rough spot in my life. But I felt I needed to open up a little here, not to point fingers or cast blame, but to say that everybody goes through painful times. And the only real hope we have is God. Turn your eyes on Him. He cares about you like no one else on earth.

EVERYBODY GOES THROUGH PAINFUL TIMES. AND THE ONLY REAL HOPE WE HAVE IS GOD.

OLD FRIEND

Oil and incense bring joy to the heart,
and the sweetness of a friend is better than self-counsel.

PROVERBS 27:9

I ran into a couple of old friends the other day. One of them I went to school with from kindergarten through the twelfth grade. He and I have known each other for a very long time, but we hadn't seen each other since high school graduation, way back in 1996.

It was such a joy to see him and catch up on people and things. Our conversation was just like people often describe: we picked up right where we'd left off. He said that since graduation, a lot of our classmates had scattered, moving away to find bigger, better jobs. That's so often the case in a small, rural community. The career opportunities just are not there, so graduates look elsewhere and the town loses lifeblood.

I told him I felt like I was the only one who had lost touch with my classmates, but he said it was the same way with him. Your life changes: you get married, and children come along, and jobs take you different places, and that closeness you once had, when everybody was in the same town going to the same school hanging out at the same places, just isn't there anymore.

I'm not on Facebook. It's just something I don't do. So getting to see my old friend's face in real life, getting to hear his voice and spending some time catching up, was sweet. He took me back to a time in my life that was free of so much responsibility and busyness; a time when I was only concerned about my schoolwork and what time to go hunting or fishing. I believe God puts people in our paths at the exact time we need them, people who will lift our spirit or put a smile on our face. God used that friend of mine to do just that.

GRATEFUL FOR MOSES

My dearly loved brothers, understand this:
Everyone must be quick to hear, slow to speak,
and slow to anger.

JAMES 1:19

I built a log cabin on our property. I call it my writing cottage. It's where I write most all of my songs. And the first one I wrote there was called "Moses." It was about my dog, my dream dog.

> He taught me patience
> Prepared me for children
> And never tried to bite anyone
> He was forgivin' no matter how I treated him
> And loved to sing us all a little song
> He was the picture of man's best friend
> Right on up until the bitter end
> Moses

I had wanted a blood-hound for as long as I can remember. So in 2004 I went to a breeder and picked out the one I wanted. I bought him when he was nine weeks old, and I named him Moses. I brought him home, gave him a bath, and then he fell asleep on my chest. From that point on we were best buddies. Moses had the sweetest spirit of any dog I'd ever been around.

Hampton and me howling with Moses

Well, Moses died six years later one September day in 2010. It was one of the saddest days in my life. I lost not only my best friend, but a good teacher. You see, Moses taught me how to be a better husband and father.

Initially, I was not a patient owner. I had a short fuse and was quick to anger. It took him awhile to break me down, but Moses finally taught me some patience. I learned that short-fuse-anger stuff had a lot more to do with my shortcomings than his. Imagine that! I can still get pretty worked up about some things, but I'm a much more mellow man these days because of him. My wife benefits daily from that, as do my boys. And they have a dog to thank—not just any dog, but a bloodhound named Moses.

For six short years he was my dream dog, my best friend. For the rest of my life I'll be a changed man.

DISCRIMINATION

Let us discern for ourselves what is right;
let us learn together what is good.

JOB 34:4 NIV

One of the hardest lessons I've had to learn is how to respond when someone critiques my work. It's hard not to take it personally! Someone can say, "Don't take it personally," but I always do. So I've had to learn not to read too many reviews. And I've grown to learn that if I've done my absolute best, then it doesn't matter what so-and-so says. I still have my moments of taking it personally, but I'm learning to rest easy after putting my heart into a song or project.

I rely heavily on my team as a strong sounding board as well. I've learned that their feedback is invaluable. If they're not feeling the words or melody, I need to pay attention. Two heads are better than one, and a team of heads has proven to be great for me.

Possibly the hardest lesson I've had to learn is how to know when to throw out the not-so-good and to keep the very good. It's the process of *discrimination*. Unfortunately that word usually carries negative connotations, but I believe it's essential for an artist. And in many ways I believe it's essential for a person in everyday life too. *Discrimination* means "to discern what is of high quality, good judgment, or taste." I have my standards; there are high bars I just won't lower. I've never settled for doing less than my best.

TEMPTATION

No temptation has overtaken you except what is common to humanity. God is faithful, and He will not allow you to be tempted beyond what you are able, but with the temptation He will also provide a way of escape so that you are able to bear it.

1 CORINTHIANS 10:13

The song that changed everything for my career was "Long Black Train." It's a song about temptation—something everybody can relate to. And my thinking is pretty black and white when it comes to the subject.

I've learned you cannot resist temptation on your own. You can try. In fact, many people have, and their stories are the stuff the tabloids and news reports are made of. I believe you need the help of the Lord and His Word to resist the temptations of this life. The verse above, found in 1 Corinthians, promises a way out. God doesn't promise that resisting temptation will be easy, but He does promise to provide a way out.

I've also realized that it's okay and completely acceptable and very wise to do away with the means of accessing whatever you're tempted by. That's not a sign of weakness at all; it's actually a sign of strength. Unsubscribe, throw it out, turn it off, whatever you have to do to keep it from being close at hand.

And if there's anything I could say about temptation, it's this: don't walk away; *run* away. Walking gives you time to reconsider, to think about it a little longer, and when you're at that point in a situation, it's usually not a good place to be. Another verse in the Bible says to "flee . . . evil" (2 Timothy 2:22 NIV). I'm pretty sure that means "Run!"

IF THERE'S
ANYTHING I
COULD SAY ABOUT
TEMPTATION, IT'S
THIS: DON'T WALK
AWAY; *RUN AWAY.*

A GOOD WIFE

A man who finds a wife finds a good thing
and obtains favor from the Lord.

PROVERBS 18:22

I dated a few girls in my younger days. I dated sorority girls, girls who didn't know the Lord, girls who came from very broken homes, girls who never really knew their daddy, even girls from New York City. All these girls had one thing in common—a wild streak. The only problem was, they didn't have it in common with me.

When Jennifer and I started dating, we were both coming off a breakup, so we were a little cautious. But the more time we spent together, the more we realized that neither of us had a wild streak in common, and that we both loved sports and music, and that we were both totally southern. I hate to admit I fell hard and fast, but boy I did!

I was visiting Jennifer's family one weekend, and I was really struggling with whether or not I should tell her my feelings. She walked upstairs as I was playing my guitar and singing "I Have Decided to Follow Jesus." When I finished she asked me to play it again, and she started singing along with me. And get this! I started crying! I really think it scared her a little, but she could see how strongly I felt about life, most of all, about her.

We've been married ten years now. In a career where people always want a piece of my time, Jennifer and I have to fight seriously for our one-on-one time with each other. We take trips and go on dates as often as we can. We've learned that if we don't, the goodness between us suffers. And that's no good. It's important, as time flies by, to remember what you have in common with each other and to keep it a priority.

MY PROPOSAL

Take wives and have sons and daughters. Take wives for
your sons and give your daughters to men in marriage
so that they may bear sons and daughters.

JEREMIAH 29:6

In 2002 I was living by myself in a 535-square-foot apartment in Nashville. I had already gotten my publishing deal, already signed my record deal, and was already in the process of putting together songs for an album. I'd even already bought a ring for Jennifer. I had a local jeweler create the ring from pictures I'd drawn and I'd kept it in my truck.

For some reason, Jennifer and I had really been on each other's nerves, arguing a lot. I kept thinking, *What's goin' on?* I had been praying about how to propose, and I had intended to do it that weekend, but with all our arguing, I thought it might be best to wait. Finally I said, "I'm tired of arguin'! We're goin' on a picnic."

Jennifer put together a basket, and we got in the truck and drove to Percy Priest Lake. We went to the boat ramp area, found a grassy spot, and put down a blanket for the basket and a CD player I'd brought along. I asked her, "Do you mind if I play you a song?"

I played "I Can See It in Your Smile," a song I'd written with Mark Narmore. Jennifer listened with tears in her eyes. I said, "I wrote it for you," and she said, "I love it."

It was a lot cooler in Nashville than usual, so I had on a jacket. I was fumbling around in the coat pocket, trying to get the ring out with one hand. I finally grabbed hold of it, held it out to her, and asked, "Will you marry me?"

Jennifer said, "Are you serious?"

I said, "Yes, I'm serious!"

Then she finally said yes to my "Will you marry me?"

That night we went to Shania Twain's album release party, and Jennifer was showing everybody the ring. The joke to this day is that Dolly Parton got to see her ring before her mama did!

MARRIAGE

Marriage should be honored by all.

HEBREWS 13:4 NIV

Jennifer and I had about five hundred people at our wedding. As we searched for a place for the ceremony, we turned down all the Baptist churches because they wouldn't let us dance afterward. We finally settled on Snellville United Methodist Church. Family, friends from the industry, everybody was there. Jennifer and I had made a recording together of "Sweet, Sweet Spirit" that played during the prelude time.

I'll never forget standing backstage with my daddy and all my groomsmen and all the thoughts running through my head. There was so much emotion going on in those moments. And when I saw Jennifer walk through that back door holding onto her daddy's arm, I lost it. The tears just started flowing. The ceremony was beautiful and powerful, just like we'd hoped. I officially committed my life to Jennifer, and she made the same commitment to me. We were starting a life together, making a covenant we vowed never to break.

It breaks my heart to see the world, as Billy Graham once said, "treating love casually." Jennifer and I take our marriage seriously. It's something worth fighting for, and we want our children to not only know that, but to see it in us. We talk to the boys a lot about the sacred union of marriage, and we believe it's important for them to see a mother and a father together the way God intended—and to be raised by both.

Jennifer and Me at *The Late Show* with David Letterman, New York City, NY, August 2012

Marriage hasn't been trouble free, but it's been beautiful and powerful. Just like we'd hoped.

AS CHRIST LOVED

Husbands, love your wives, just as Christ loved the church
and gave Himself for her.

EPHESIANS 5:25

Sometimes I feel that verse could just as easily read, "Husbands, *learn* your wives." Maybe a commitment to learning is really the only way to love. I know I've had to learn my wife. I'll explain.

Jennifer is gentle and kind; in other words, very sensitive. That's who God created her to be. If she were different, she wouldn't be Jennifer. So I've had to learn to be gentle and kind with her. Now that's not who I naturally am; I have a tendency to, well, not be so gentle or kind at times. But if I'm serious about loving Jennifer—and I am—then I'll set aside my natural tendencies and seek to love her as she's been created. It's what that verse means when it says "gave Himself for her."

Another thing, Jennifer likes little handwritten notes. Now I didn't start out being very good at small, handwritten notes. But I've learned, and you know what? I'm pretty good at it now. It's just another way, regardless of how small, that I show her my love for her is serious, that my "I love you" really means something.

So, husbands, don't claim to *love* your wife if you're not willing to *learn* her. Your claims won't be believable to those around you or, most important of all, to your wife. Jesus is our example in this: He knows us, and He loves us.

HUSBANDS, DON'T CLAIM TO *LOVE* YOUR WIFE IF YOU'RE NOT WILLING TO *LEARN HER.*

LET IT SHINE

"Bring the full tenth into the storehouse so that there may
be food in My house. Test Me in this way," says the Lord of
Hosts. "See if I will not open the floodgates of heaven
and pour out a blessing for you without measure."

MALACHI 3:10

Some folks may not think the Bible says much about money, but it actually does. The Bible consistently teaches that you don't give in order to get more; you give in gratitude for what God has already given you. There's a difference there. A big difference.

I've been very blessed, with my wife, family, career, talent, and friends. As I think about my life, these old song lyrics come to mind: *This little light of mine, I'm gonna let it shine.* I always want to give back to God, to let my light shine in that way. I know all the blessings in Josh Turner's life are due to God's mercy and grace. I never want to hide my gratitude under a bushel.

And it was really because somebody else didn't hide her thankfulness that I learned to do the same. Her name was

Sue Carol Poston. She was my Sunday school teacher for a few years and my third-grade teacher at Hannah Elementary. Every Sunday like clockwork, she'd pull out her checkbook before class started and give forty dollars to the church. This happened every Sunday without fail.

It's true that the Bible teaches about giving tithes and offerings. But I saw that principle faithfully lived out in the flesh-and-blood example of my Sunday school teacher. Letting her light shine in the form of that forty dollars check made a difference in my life. A big difference.

LISTEN AND BELIEVE

Listen, my son, and be wise.

PROVERBS 23:19

There's a lot to be said for listening to a good doctor. There's also a lot to be said for listening to your body. And sometimes they're telling you two different things.

Years ago I had this awful pain in my side. I had done everything I knew to get rid of it but to no avail. I went to one doctor's office, had blood work done, and was told I was fine. The only problem was, my body was telling me I wasn't fine. So I went to another doctor, this time one who was willing to search for the root of the problem. He discovered I had chronic inflammation in my gut due to stress, the way I was eating, and generally not taking good care of myself. If I had stopped after that first misdiagnosis of "fine," I could have ended up in more pain and with significantly more problems. So listen to your body.

But there's another angle to this, and that's believing in your body and its incredible capacity to heal itself if you allow it to.

Another time a doctor diagnosed me with spinal stenosis. I was told I would not be able to play basketball or lift weights or do many of the things I truly loved to do. But I refused to believe that I couldn't get better. I'm the father of three boys, and I wanted to play sports with them and wrestle with them. I had to get better.

I managed to find a good chiropractor, one who was very communicative with me, took x-rays, told me what kind of treatment I needed, told me why this was going on; basically explained everything to me. I learned that everyone is supposed to have a 43-degree curvature in their neck. When the doctor showed me my x-rays, he pointed out that I had a 6-degree curvature in my neck. That difference was causing all kinds of problems, from neck pain to headaches, discomfort, and maybe even some of the sinus problems I'd had. That difference kept me from doing a lot of the things I loved to do. It had affected my singing and caused a lot of tension and stress in my neck and shoulder area.

So under the guidance of this good chiropractor, I started in on a plan and immediately began feeling a lot better. About five months later I had new x-rays taken: my neck curvature had improved to 17 degrees! This was so encouraging to me that I refused to believe ever again that my body couldn't heal itself. All because this one doctor took the time to properly diagnose the problem and help me get better.

Listen to your body *and* believe in your body. Those two practices are invaluable when it comes to the quality of life you desire to live.

ENEMY ACTION

Be serious! Be alert! Your adversary the Devil is prowling around
like a roaring lion, looking for anyone he can devour.

1 PETER 5:8

I grew up playing sports and working on the farm and doing all kinds of things outdoors. So you'd think I'd have a history of broken arms and legs and wrists and ribs and toes. But that's not the case. The injuries I've sustained have predominantly been from the neck up.

My war wounds have included my sister hitting me in the head with a brick and me chipping my teeth as my jaws clamped together when our school bus hit a pothole. Then there was the time I flipped over my bicycle handlebars while at Mamama's house and *broke* my jaw. Then I got whiplash after a horse I was riding got spooked and bolted, I got my nose broken in a basketball game, and then there was a recent diagnosis of spinal stenosis. That's just a sampling of my injuries!

Somebody might think that was just a lot of bad luck. But I believe all those injuries and the rest were strategic attempts by the enemy to stop me from singing, from using my God-given talents here on earth. Each of those injuries has affected my voice and my singing. And most all of them have dulled my spirit as well. If I were a baseball pitcher and the enemy wanted to take me out, I could see getting injuries to my hands or eyesight. If I were a track star, I would expect the attacks to be aimed at my feet and legs. But I'm not either of those. I'm a singer, so injuries from the neck up are, in my opinion, much more than coincidence. They are evidence that we live this life opposed, that we have an enemy, and that we need to live alert. Don't give the devil too much credit but do recognize when he's trying to keep you from doing what God has called you to.

DON'T GIVE THE DEVIL TOO MUCH CREDIT BUT DO RECOGNIZE WHEN HE'S TRYING TO KEEP YOU FROM DOING WHAT GOD HAS CALLED YOU TO.

GETTING IN ON THE PLANS

"For I know the plans I have for you"—this is
the LORD's declaration—"plans for your welfare, not
for disaster, to give you a future and a hope."

JEREMIAH 29:11

The best and worst year of my life? That's easy: 2004.

I was probably gone from home three hundred days that year. I was having anxiety and heart issues due to all the stress. Plus, all the ibuprofen I was taking for the headaches from all the stress caused extreme inflammation in my gut. That was a year when it would have been really easy to give up and quit. It was just too much.

There were a lot of offers coming in but I didn't feel like I had much say about what was being accepted and what was being rejected. And when you're first starting out, not all of the offers you get are good. So, while I was happy to be getting work, the demands on me and my health were taking their toll. It was also my first full year of marriage, and Jennifer and I had decided that she would come on the road with me. But even with that, the fifty or so days we were home were spent doing everything from running errands to grocery shopping to writing songs. It was completely insane. I swore I'd never do that again.

To add to the stress, it became apparent to me that I needed to make some big decisions about taking steps to put a new team in place, which was not easy. One *good* thing that helped me was my favorite verse in the Bible: Jeremiah 29:11. It's not so much that I held on to that verse that year, but that verse held on to me. God's plans were to prosper me, not harm me. And that "not harm" part would lead to a hopeful future. But God wanted me to agree with His plan by stepping up and saying, "Yeah, that's good" and "No, that'll never happen again."

MAN TEARS

Jesus wept.

JOHN 11:35

If you were to ask me if it's okay for a man to cry, I'd say, "It depends on what kind of man you are." Just like there are different kinds of fish in the river, there are different kinds of men on the earth. Take my daddy, for instance. He's a numbers kind of man, he couldn't care less about style or fashion, and he doesn't wear his heart on his sleeve. Because of that, I haven't seen him shed too many tears.

But my mama's daddy? Now he was pretty emotional. In fact, he was what you'd call a romantic. I saw him shed a lot of tears.

Then take me. For whatever reason, I'm more artsy, creative, and very sensitive to my emotions and those of others around me. You might call me a romantic too. I've never been ashamed of shedding a tear. I see it as just another way of expressing emotion, of being human.

Jesus had a trusted friend named Lazarus who got sick and died. If you know anything about that story, you know that Jesus called His friend out of the grave and resurrected him from the dead. It was truly a miracle. But if you jump to the miracle too fast, as we sometimes have a tendency to do, you miss the tears Jesus shed at the tomb. I'm sure those tears represent a number of emotions that were going on inside Jesus. But at the very least, those tears expressed His unashamed humanity.

I don't know if Jesus felt He had to cry at the tomb of His good friend, but I do know He didn't stop Himself. So if shedding tears is okay by Jesus, then it's okay by me.

I DON'T KNOW IF
JESUS FELT HE HAD
TO CRY AT THE
TOMB OF HIS GOOD
FRIEND, BUT I DO
KNOW HE DIDN'T
STOP HIMSELF.

A FATHER'S BLESSINGS

Like arrows in the hand of a warrior
are the sons born in one's youth.
Happy is the man who has filled his quiver with them.

PSALM 127:4–5

The births of our three sons have been moments of sheer joy. Don't get me wrong, there was labor involved, obviously. But I've learned that most things worth doing are hard. And that goes for children: bringing them into this world as well as raisin' them.

Hampton was almost three years old when Colby was born. He was old enough to know that Jennifer was pregnant and he was gonna have a little brother. The day Colby was born, Hampton stayed overnight with my brother and his wife, and they brought Hampton to the hospital the next morning. I have to say, watching Hampton eye his newborn brother was the most innocent and precious thing I think I've ever seen. It was a magical moment.

As a father, I try to keep those moments fresh in my mind. Those are moments when I'm aware of just how very blessed I am.

A PRAYER FOR MY SONS

Pour out your heart like water
before the Lord's presence.
Lift up your hands to Him
for the lives of your children.

LAMENTATIONS 2:19

Have you ever considered writing a prayer for your children? I think it's a good idea because it forces you to really think about what you're praying about and what you're saying to or asking God for on their behalf. Not only that, your children can look back on the prayer (or prayers) years from now and see how God answered.

Here's a prayer I wrote for my boys not long ago.

Dear Lord,

I love my sons. I pray they will grow to become great men for You, stable in their own lives, able to stand on their own two feet while always leanin' on Your everlastin' arms.

I pray for their future, Lord, that they will chase the dreams You've given them. Help them to realize at an early age what those dreams are and what their destiny is. I know what an advantage it was for me to have a sense of Your plans early on. I pray You will lead them in that same way. Lead them as they pursue their education and college and even where they'll live, all of those things that factor into the careers You have for them.

Lord, I pray for their wives, the girls they will marry one day in the future. I pray for those girls even now, that they will grow to know who You are and have a personal relationship with You, Jesus. I know how important, how absolutely necessary, it is for a husband and wife to be grounded in You, Lord.

I pray for my sons' protection and for their safety. I realize I can't obsess over this. They are in Your hands. Jennifer and I have them for a time. Guide us as we strive to raise them in a godly home, givin' them the tools they'll need to leave the nest and go out on their own. We want them to be prepared for that, Lord, to know who You are and who they are, and to know that Jennifer and I love them from the very bottom of our hearts.

In Jesus' name I pray.

Amen.

WHAT'S IN A NAME?

A good name is to be chosen over great wealth;
favor is better than silver and gold.

PROVERBS 22:1

I am the father of three boys. They each have good names, names that mean something.

My oldest son is Hampton Otis, named after Civil War general Wade Hampton of South Carolina. He was the governor of South Carolina, an outdoorsman, and physically strong. *Otis* was part of my granny's daddy's name—Quincy Otis Wise. Also my middle name is Otis, after my daddy.

My middle son is Colby Lynch. I grew up on Lynches River, so I originally wanted his name to be *Lynch* but realized it really wasn't a first name. *Colby* means "coal miner's settlement," but another interpretation is "man of the outdoors." I knew Colby's name was a fit the first time he picked up a lizard: he didn't even flinch.

My youngest son is Crawford Marion, named after the Revolutionary War hero Francis Marion, known to have kept the colonies inspired. The story goes that at a big party in

Charleston, the owner of the house barred all the doors and told everyone, "Alright, nobody's going home until we all get drunk!" Wanting no part of that, Francis Marion jumped out the top-floor window, broke his leg upon landing, and limped all the way home. Later that evening the British came by and burned the home and all the drunken occupants in it. The name *Crawford* means "the crossing of blood lines," and it has the word *ford* in it, which is Jennifer's maiden name.

I am the father of three boys. I pray that they grow into their names, and that the lives they choose to live will have a positive impact on someone else's.

Historical marker, Hannah, SC

THE MOUTHS OF BABES

I never stop giving thanks for you as I remember you in my prayers.

EPHESIANS 1:16

One thing I've been trying to teach my boys lately is that the best thing you can tell a soldier is "Thank you for servin' our country!"

Well, recently our family was in a restaurant in Washington, DC, where we saw some soldiers eating, so I urged Hampton to walk over and speak to them. Since he was a little nervous, Colby went with him for moral support. So off they went together, and Hampton said exactly what I had been teaching him to say to a soldier: "Thank you for servin' our country!" Those soldiers smiled and gave my sons high fives.

Six little words out of the mouths of babes changed that place from just a restaurant that served food to a place that honored the brave sacrifices our men and women in the military are making every day so you and I can live free. Approaching strangers and expressing your appreciation may not always be the easiest thing to do, and sometimes having a brother or friend along for moral support is needed, but showing a little gratitude is the least we can do in return for the freedom we have in our country.

SHOWING A LITTLE GRATITUDE IS THE LEAST WE CAN DO IN RETURN FOR THE FREEDOM WE HAVE IN OUR COUNTRY.

A PLACE OF LOVE

The one who will not use the rod hates his son,
but the one who loves him disciplines him diligently.

PROVERBS 13:24

The very first spanking of my life happened before my brother and sister were even born. My parents and I were outside, and they said, "Don't go out to the highway." They turned around to do whatever it was they were doing, and guess where I headed?

When my parents turned back around, I was exactly where they had told me not to go. Not only was I beyond their reach, I was standing not in the middle of some dirt back road, but in the middle of Highway 378! That little trip earned me the first and worst spanking of my life!

It's true that sparing the rod spoils the child. Another way of saying it is, not sparing the rod saves the child. The middle of that highway was a dangerous place for me. I could have been severely injured or even killed. And my parents' discipline came from their love for me. Their correction saved me on that occasion, as well as many others.

A twisted sort of discipline comes from a place of hate. There is no justification for that, ever. But the careful actions that the writer of Proverbs talked about is born from a place of love. I learned that lesson as a boy, and I am learning it again as a father.

DON'T NEGOTIATE

The Lord disciplines the one He loves,
just as a father, the son he delights in.

PROVERBS 3:12

One of the expectations my boys have of me is discipline. I've made a promise to discipline them, and if I can't keep that promise, even when it's painful, then I can't be depended on to keep the easy promises either. As far as punishment goes, if I feel like they deserve correction, I give it.

I remember a woman at my daddy's bank asking him, "What's your secret to having well-behaved children?" He said, "I don't negotiate with them." I've adopted that philosophy. Nip it in the bud; don't let it drag on.

Jennifer helps me with this, though, by making sure the punishment matches the crime. Sometimes it's hard to decide what punishment to give and whether the consequences should be light, medium, or heavy. This does get a little easier the older they get because we can talk about it and sometimes talk it out. I want my sons to respect me as well as love me.

I take being a father seriously, and I strive to be good at it. I also take pride in it, the good kind of pride, the kind that says to God, "Thank You for my children."

I WANT MY SONS TO RESPECT ME AS WELL AS LOVE ME.

RUN TOWARD LOVE

First go and be reconciled to them.

MATTHEW 5:24 NIV

When I was a boy, there was nothing I hated worse than my daddy's belt. I can remember a few times when we'd put on four or five pairs of pants because we knew the belt was coming. My parents made us strip down to our underwear, then get the spanking. Sometimes Mama would spank the moment we did something wrong, and then when Daddy got home, we'd get the second wave.

One time when we were with my mama's parents and I got in trouble with Daddy, he spanked me in their presence. But here's something: even though my granddaddy reached out his arms to console me, I ran to my daddy's arms instead. That might sound strange, but even as children, we run toward reconciliation; we'll run toward love. It's important for children to know the answer to this simple question: "Do you still love me?"

I keep that in mind when I need to punish my boys. I believe that afterward, just like me, they want to know the answer to "Do you still love me?" And the answer is the same as the one my daddy always gave: "Yes."

IT'S IMPORTANT FOR CHILDREN TO KNOW THE ANSWER TO THIS SIMPLE QUESTION: "DO YOU STILL LOVE ME?"

WITH ME

Jesus went with them.

LUKE 7:6

One of the best ways my daddy bestowed masculinity on me and taught me important life lessons was by being engaged: he did things *with* me. On Saturday mornings we'd go to Hardee's for sausage biscuits and orange juice, and he would eat *with* me. Some Saturdays we'd get in his one-man boat and go to Lynches River, and Daddy would fish all day long *with* me. We might find a sandbar and eat and swim; again, my daddy would do these things *with* me.

As parents you and I want to do things *for* our children. But as you go along, you discover they'd much rather do most of those things for themselves. What they want from you, even though they may not know it, is for you to do things *with* them. Don't make it forced or orchestrated, but natural. Remember, your goal is not to be profound. Your goal is to be a parent.

It doesn't matter whether or not you have a lot of money. What matters is that you take care of what you have. And I learned that the best way to take care of children is to be *with* them.

TOGETHERNESS

I will boast in the Lord;
the humble will hear and be glad.
Proclaim Yahweh's greatness with me;
let us exalt His name together.

PSALM 34:2–3

"One thing I noticed was that Josh knows so much about his boys. Most guys don't; they're working all the time. Josh knows them inside and out." That comment was made about me recently. I don't see it as anything out of the ordinary, but I do know my boys.

And I don't know them by accident. Years ago Jennifer and I decided we would travel together as a family. And as our family has grown, we've stayed committed to that decision. After sharing moments on stage with Jennifer (she's part of the band), we're greeted at the tour bus doors by our boys. No matter how the show may go, I forget all about that when I get to the bus and start playing with them.

Some people might not agree with this approach of having the boys on the road, but I believe it gives them an advantage.

They'll be extremely well-rounded, well-balanced, and well-traveled. It's fun for me to see my boys learn about the country we live in and about the people—the good, the bad, and the ugly—who live here.

I feel very fortunate about having a job that allows me to spend as much time with my boys as I do—I know that many jobs don't allow fathers to do the same, so I feel very blessed. We travel together, and we're a happy family. And Hampton has had some really great show-and-tells for his class when we come back from touring.

Hampton, Colby, Marion, and me, Lee's Summit, MO

Then God said, "Let Us make man in Our image, according
to Our likeness. They will rule the fish of the sea, the birds
of the sky, the livestock, all the earth, and the creatures
that crawl on the earth." So God created man in His
own image; He created him in the image of God.

GENESIS 1:26–27

The other day I had a discussion with a friend about how
children from the same parents can be so different from
one another. I think those differences are clear evidence of the
fact that God is a multifaceted artist. As His Word says, we are
created "in His own image," but what a wide range of people
we are! If you stop and consider how many people there are
in the world, and how each and every person is completely
different from the other, it shows how many different personality traits God has. As a father, I have noticed firsthand
how children with the same DNA can be so very different. I've
seen it in my three boys. Although they have some physical
similarities (they tend to look alike at certain phases of their
lives) and certain mannerisms, at the same time the boys are
completely different from one another.

Take Hampton for example. He just turned seven and is our oldest. Hampton is very creative and very poetic. He loves to draw, he loves music, and he is very sensitive and emotional at times. He really has a romantic's heart.

Then there's our four-year-old, Colby. Colby is laid back and easygoing: there's just not a lot that rattles him. Right now he doesn't care at all about his ABCs or his 123s; he is the child who asks the deep questions. Colby is our thinker, so he's very good at being still and quiet.

And then there's Marion, our battering ram, no-holds-barred, monster truck-loving two-year-old who loves to tear stuff up and make a mess. Marion also loves to laugh. He's an absolute entertainer/comedian whose great sense of humor is already apparent. As the third child he tries to mimic his older brothers, so he has some Hampton and Colby traits in him. But his individuality is impossible to miss: Marion is Marion.

I love seeing how very different my boys are. Right here in my own backyard is clear evidence of how we're all unique, created in the image of God.

WITHOUT HIM

May the Lord of peace Himself give you peace always
in every way. The Lord be with all of you.

2 THESSALONIANS 3:16

The story goes that as a seventeen-year-old, he was stationed at Fort Jackson, South Carolina. His family had a music gig in Memphis, so he hitchhiked from the base to Memphis, and his family let him sing a song he had just written. His name was Mylon LeFevre, and the song was titled "Without Him."

That night on the side of the stage was another artist who heard the song and loved it. He then went on to record it. His name was Elvis Presley.

Years ago some friends and I formed a gospel quartet. We called ourselves The Thankful Hearts. One of the first songs we learned to sing and perform was "Without Him." It is my favorite hymn because it speaks so strongly of peace and encouragement.

I sing that song to my children each night. My two-year-old has now grown to expect it, and I love that. He even sings along with me. The last line in the song is the perfect ending thought for our days: *Without Him how lost I would be.*

THE BIG TRIP

Take delight in the LORD,
and He will give you your heart's desires.

PSALM 37:4

For our tenth wedding anniversary, Jennifer and I took a trip to the Big Island of Hawaii. It was somewhat of a splurge for us, but we knew we wanted to go somewhere neither of us had ever been. Jennifer and I are somewhat different when it comes to vacations. If we go to a beach, for instance, she wants to sit on the beach, and that's pretty much it. I, on the other hand, want to get out and explore and see what's around. I want to experience as much of the place I'm in as possible.

On this trip we did a little of both. On some days we just sat around, but on other days we got out and saw the island. We ended up pretty much seeing the entire island. It was truly an incredible trip. Over the course of those days, we had a lot of time to talk and pray together and think and relax. It was so good for us to get away, just the two of us, getting to know each other again.

One of the things we did on a get-out-and-see-things day

Jennifer and me on Punalu'u black sand beach, Pahala, HI

was to travel to the little town of Hawi (pronounced *Ha-vee*). I had been told that Hawi was the best place to buy ukuleles, and I'd always wanted a ukulele. It was a desire of my heart. Well, we found a shop there, and I actually ended up buying two—one old (1969) and the other, brand-new. While on our trip, I learned a few chords and ended up writing the song "Hawaiian Girl."

We saw valleys and waterfalls, flew over macadamia nut orchards and coffee plantations, and walked on black sand beaches. We even ended up one evening at an astronomy center on Mauna Kea, where we looked through telescopes and saw the rings of Saturn and a satellite orbiting the earth.

We're grateful that we were able to get away and celebrate ten years of marriage. We became closer to each other and to God—and we can't wait to go back!

WISDOM AND FOOLISHNESS

Put on the full armor of God so that you can
stand against the tactics of the Devil.

EPHESIANS 6:11

This is a story about Mamama—that's my mama's mama. She was the choir director at Union Baptist Church in Hannah, South Carolina, for almost forty years. Mamama was completely devoted to the church and the people who served there. One of those people was me: that's the church I grew up in.

Several years ago there was a crisis in that church. It revolved around the preacher, who had done some things that were not acceptable to the people of the church. Eventually everything came to a point where the church was going to put it to a vote—either keep him or not. Word about "the vote" got out into the community, and certain individuals tried to get as many people as they could to show up and vote their way. It was, as situations like that often are, dishonest.

The big day came and a lot of people showed up who didn't normally go to church on a regular basis. One of these

ladies passed by Mamama, and their exchange went something like this:

Lady: "Hello."

Mamama: "It's good to see you here."

Lady: "It sounds like the devil is in the church, so we came
to help out."

Mamama: "The devil's always been in the church."

I was impressed with Mamama being so quick on her feet,
but I was more impressed with what she said. I'd never really
thought of it that way before, but she was absolutely right. The
devil has always been in the church trying to stir up dissen-
sion and divide God's people. The devil knows God's Word
and uses distortions of it against us Christians. Mamama
knew that; the other lady did not. And that's at least one difference between wisdom and foolishness.

LOVE THE SINNER

Love must be without hypocrisy. Detest evil; cling to what is good.

ROMANS 12:9

You've probably heard the statement before: hate the sin; love the sinner. I think all of us Christians struggle with that, but sometimes it's really a challenge for me. I've faced situations in my life where I've *had* to love the sinner because the sinner was family. But when someone returns that love, you realize it's the right way, the way things should be.

It's a pretty heavy thing, though. I saw a family member get caught up in a sinful lifestyle several years ago. My family took him in, but they also let him know they did not condone what he was doing. I was younger at the time, but I saw firsthand how significant my family's treatment was for him. I'm so glad they didn't kick him out or shun him. The rest of the story is that God has brought a lot of restoration to that situation. And I believe a small part of that restoring is due to my family living the way we as Christians are supposed to live.

Hate the sin; love the sinner. It's not easy, but it's right.

NEVER STOP

We must not get tired of doing good,
for we will reap at the proper time if we don't give up.

GALATIANS 6:9

When it comes to mentors, I've found that having one is not like what the movies show. It's usually not just one person mentoring, but several, each one contributing something different to your life. I've got a handful of mentors in my life: my daddy, Jennifer's daddy, and a couple of close friends. But it was still hard because I'd never connected with anybody older than me who's been down the road I'm on and reached out to me or taken me under his wing. Well, nobody besides John.

John Anderson had long been a musical hero of mine. He has been not only a musical mentor to me but a life mentor. He saw "Long Black Train" on Country Music Television (CMT) and invited me to come out to his house to meet him. It was like we'd known each other all our lives. He fried some shrimp, and we sat around talking and singing songs back and forth to each other. There were several times that day I had to stop and tell myself, "Man, I'm sittin' here with John Anderson!"

I called John after I lost the third single of my career. By that I mean the song just sorta died on the charts. Never a good thing. He told me about some song he'd put out that died way down somewhere on the charts too. But he also told me that the next song was the biggest of his career. He said: "Don't get too caught up on the one that failed. Keep writin'. Never stop the ball from rollin'."

John Anderson and me in the studio, Nashville, TN

I've always wanted to use my talent to do good; to help somebody feel better is my goal. So I took John's advice not to give up. The next song I released was "Your Man," and let's just say, it didn't die on the charts!

FAVORITES

They sing to the music of timbrel and lyre;
they make merry to the sound of the pipe.

JOB 21:12 NIV

A s a father I don't love any one of my sons more than the other two, but I do love them differently. As a student of country music, I don't have a favorite song I love more than the rest. But I do have a handful I love differently because each one speaks to me in a certain way.

Vern Gosdin was known as "The Voice." His song "Is It Raining at Your House?" is one of my favorites. Then I have another favorite: "I'm No Stranger to the Rain" by Keith Whitley.

Two of my mentors are Randy Travis and John Anderson. Randy's "Out of My Bones" and John's "Wish I Could Have Been There" make the list of my favorite songs.

I know it's dangerous to point to any one country music artist and say, "I love all his songs!" But dangerous or not, I feel that way about the music of Hank Williams.

One common thread in all these songs is that the artists behind them were and are committed to the roots of country music. And roots are important to me, both as a student of country music and as a father.

LEARNING FROM OTHERS

I saw, and took it to heart;
I looked, and received instruction.

PROVERBS 24:32

I have what I call a Mount Rushmore of Country Music. The faces and lives of these men are pronounced in my career. I have learned from their successes as well as their mistakes.

Randy Travis taught me early on how to maintain my image, both commercial and country.

John Anderson taught me how to be a vocal stylist, how to write my own songs, and how to be true to myself.

Vern Gosdin taught me how to evoke emotion through a song.

Johnny Cash taught me how to sing and write with meaning.

And Hank Williams was my template. He set the standard for country songwriting; he taught me that there's power and truth in a simple song.

Randy Travis and me at Randy's Walk of Fame induction, Nashville, TN

WRITING THE SONGS

My heart is moved by a noble theme
as I recite my verses to the king;
my tongue is the pen of a skillful writer.

PSALM 45:1

People ask me all the time about my songwriting process. First, I start with an idea. My ideas come from anywhere and everywhere. I'm always looking for and storing away ideas, twists of phrases (everyday phrases you'd hear somebody say), interesting concepts, stories, and title suggestions. I never know where a great song is going to come from, so I'm always listening, watching. Even if some ideas seem too silly or sound overly serious, I'm always open to them because you just never know what might transpire.

When it comes to the number of ideas I need, there can never be too many. Fortunately I've managed to have more ideas than songs, and that's the way I prefer it. I've found that when you run out of ideas, it's really hard to write because the idea is the starting point: it's the seed the song tree grows from. So I'm always writing down my ideas and making notes. I don't want to miss the seed.

When it comes to the actual writing, I go to my writing cottage to block out all distractions. (The cottage has no phone, TV, or Internet service.) Sometimes I write by myself, and sometimes I cowrite. If I'm cowriting, another writer will come over, and we'll sit down and bounce ideas off each other until we find one we both get fired up about. From there we just start looking and listening within ourselves for the melody that perfectly fits the title or song idea. Sometimes we tailor the melody to what we think it should be, and sometimes the melody kinda comes out on its own. Those are the magical times of songwriting! You just never know where your efforts will lead.

And then there are those days when we finish working on a song, listen to it, and think, *Oh, it's not very good at all.* Then on other days the opposite happens: when we've been working on a song so long, we can't tell whether it's got what we've been aiming for or not. So we step away for a little while, come back to it, and say, "Wow, we wrote a really good song today." When that happens, it is truly gratifying. It's magical, but it's not magic.

I believe that great songs come from another realm, and I'm always praying that God will allow me to tap into it.

"WHY, SHORE, SON!"

Don't neglect to show hospitality, for by doing this some have welcomed angels as guests without knowing it.

HEBREWS 13:2

Jerry Clower was a huge hero of mine when I was a boy. My family saw him do a show at a warehouse during the Tobacco Festival in Lake City, South Carolina, and we had a great time. After the show we all went to Country Cousins Bar-B-Que in Scranton for supper. We pulled up in the parking lot, and all of a sudden a long, white Cadillac pulled up. Daddy said, "Look at that." We watched as Jerry got out of the Cadillac. And there he stood—in all his glory—wearing that red suit of his with the raccoons all over it!

I just had to try and get his autograph. Mama gave me a pencil and tore off the corner of a page of notebook paper. When I ran over to him and asked, he said, "Why, shore, son!" Jerry Clower didn't know me from Adam, but he gave me the autograph I asked for. And I kept that autograph on the refrigerator for a long time. Then it just disappeared. I still don't know what happened to it. I'd give a million dollars for that autograph right now—it was that special.

Now I'm the one performing, and I want to always treat my fans the way Jerry Clower treated me that night outside Country Cousins Bar-B-Que. He was hospitable, he treated me with kindness, and I have never forgotten the great impression he made on me.

TAKE CARE

Do you not know that your bodies are temples of the Holy Spirit,
who is in you, whom you have received from God?

1 CORINTHIANS 6:19 NIV

Around the time Marion was born, I did a photo shoot for *People* magazine. Up to that point I'd felt like I was in pretty good physical shape, but I wasn't happy when I saw those pictures. The truth is, I'd let myself go; I didn't look healthy.

So I started doing push-ups and sit-ups every day and eating really clean. Almost immediately I noticed my body responding to the discipline. And I remembered how much I loved exercising. I had forgotten how much it meant to me and how good I felt when I was consistent with an exercise routine.

Not long after getting into better shape, I was at the airport and ran into a guy named Rich Froning. Rich is a three-time CrossFit Games champion, and I'd seen him in *Muscle & Fitness* magazine. We visited awhile and I really felt like CrossFit was what I was supposed to do at the time. So I transformed our garage into a CrossFit gym, and now Jennifer and I work out

Rich Froning and me at the Nashville International Airport

regularly. I feel very good to be back in shape and taking care of my body.

I've found that people can be obsessive about working out or, to the other extreme, lazy. The trick is finding the middle ground: eat clean, train hard, and stick with the discipline of being consistent. Your body is a temple for the Holy Spirit, and you can take care of it and keep it presentable, or you can let it go and face the consequences. But the truth is, Jennifer and I don't do this just for our own satisfaction. We want to be good examples for our boys. When they see us taking care of our bodies, hopefully they'll grow up to take care of theirs.

STICK WITH WHAT YOU LOVE

Faithful love and truth will join together;
righteousness and peace will embrace.

PSALM 85:10

My daddy's always been a basketball fan. He loves the sport. As you can guess, he taught me about basketball, and I learned to play pretty well. In fact, I made the varsity team when I was in the eighth grade. But for years the coach refused to play me. In his eyes, I couldn't do anything right. Everyone else wondered, "Why won't you play Josh?" I did all the right things in practice, but I never got to play.

Finally, in my junior year, I realized it was a matter of discrimination, and I wasn't the only victim. Two of my friends actually quit the team earlier that season. While constantly sitting on the bench was hard on me, it killed my daddy, especially since he knew I was pretty good. Although Daddy was discouraged, he encouraged me to stick with it.

Well, the straw that broke the camel's back was a game against North Myrtle Beach, and to everyone's surprise (mainly mine), the coach started me! I scored the first four points of the game, but after that second shot, he took me out. And I stayed out for the rest of the game. When the fourth quarter started and I wasn't back on the floor, I'd had enough. I walked back to the locker room, changed clothes, then went back to sit with my parents. You could have heard a pin drop in that gym. Everyone knew I'd finally quit.

Years later, that high school coach attended a show of mine in, ironically, North Myrtle Beach! He ran into my daddy in the parking lot of the venue and asked him if he could get backstage to see me. My daddy is a man of few words and that moment was no exception. He simply said, "No."

I still play basketball to this day. Like my daddy, I love the sport. I could have let that high school experience scar me, but I didn't. A part of the reason why was because of my daddy and his constant encouragement. Stick with what you love, regardless of what the person in charge does or doesn't do. And if you decide to quit the team, it doesn't have to mean you quit the game.

ON THE ROAD

When the LORD had finished speaking with Abraham,
He departed, and Abraham returned to his place.

GENESIS 18:33

B eing on the road for many years has taught me a few things. First off, it's mind-boggling just how big this country we call America is. The diversity of the terrain is simply amazing. There's a big world out there, and I believe we should try to see as much of it as we can. Every part is different and beautiful in its own way. For instance, there's the strength of the Mississippi River, and then there's the majesty of the Smokey Mountains. There's the culture of a place like San Antonio, Texas, and then if you drive a few days, you can take in the wonder of a place like Yellowstone National Park. The vastness makes you feel small, but in a good way, a humbling way.

That goes for the people too. People are very different throughout the country. People in Seattle, Washington, are different from those in Joplin, Missouri. They have different perspectives on everything from food to sports. But there's one connection that overrides the differences, and that's when a person is a Christian. It's a different kind of beauty to see how comfortable people can be around one another because of that common thread.

The second thing I've learned is that, while I love traveling and being able to play for so many fans, being away makes you appreciate home even more. I've learned that when you're thousands of miles away, that old saying is absolutely right: *There's no place like home.*

My daddy has said, "I don't know how y'all do this, movin' on a bus all the time." For him living like that would cause a spirit of unrest. I understand this. Over many years and even more miles, we've learned it's very important to be able to have a place to come home to, a place where we feel we belong, where we can let our hair down and be real people, where we can retreat and rest and recharge.

It's like two sides of a coin. One is the going out and traveling far; the other is the heading back toward home. Both are necessary. One without the other leaves your life shortchanged.

GIVING FORWARD

"You have received free of charge; give free of charge."

JESUS IN MATTHEW 10:8

I attended a small, rural high school that didn't have much as far as music and the arts were concerned. I wouldn't trade that experience for anything because it had a lot of other benefits, but I do wish some things had been different. Because of that wish, I'd long had the desire to help students in high schools like the one I attended, to help them go on to college and major in music and the arts.

So in 2005 Jennifer and I started the Josh Turner Scholarship Fund. There have been five recipients so far. It's been very satisfying to know we're helping someone get somewhere they might not have if we hadn't helped. Initially the scope was small, but now we've expanded the offer to the entire state of South Carolina. Our hope is that in the next five years, the scholarship will be available to students across the entire United States.

I've worked very hard in my career, and I've been blessed along the way. It's very important to me to give back in a variety of ways, and the scholarship fund is one of those ways. It's giving back, but it's also a way of giving forward, of doing what I can to help students make their dreams a reality.

The second Josh Turner Scholarship Fund recipient, Cameron Turner (no relation) and me on stage, Alabama Theater, North Myrtle Beach, SC

LONG TIME COMING

Endurance must do its complete work,
so that you may be mature and complete, lacking nothing.

JAMES 1:4

Every now and then I hear people use their age as an excuse for not being able to do something well or reach a goal. I believe that as long as you have a positive mind-set, and you're focused and determined and persistent, you can accomplish great things in your life no matter your age.

As a boy I was really strong for my size. I worked on the farm, played sports, and lifted weights in the garage. I've always had that tall, thin body type, what some people call "the skinny guy." But I was strong. I enjoyed lifting weights, so much so that when I went to Francis Marion University my first year (in 1996), I took a weight lifting class. It was during that class that I was trying to max out on my bench press. To "max out" simply means to reach the maximum amount of weight you can press for one repetition.

I had worked up to 195 pounds on the bar and felt like I could make it an even 200. That's just five pounds, right? So a couple of my classmates put a 2.5-pound plate on each end, and I gave it a try. And I couldn't press it. They took off one of the 2.5-pound plates, and I could get the 197.5 pounds. But for whatever reason, I could not get past that point. I could not bench press 200 pounds.

I transferred to Belmont University in 1998 with a 110 percent focus on my music. I ate, slept, and breathed music—every day, all the time. As a result, I slacked off on my physical, active lifestyle. This lasted for quite a while. I got my first record deal in 2001, got married in 2003, and those first couple years of touring were nothing like my younger days when I was in shape.

In the past two-and-a-half years, I've been consistent and determined about staying healthy, eating right, working out, really trying to take care of myself. A part of this recommitment to fitness has been working on that old challenge of bench pressing 200 pounds. In April of 2013, I benched 190 pounds. I had worked back up to that weight. It was difficult, but I made it. One month later I benched 195 pounds, and I was there—right back at that same spot I had been seventeen years earlier: five pounds shy of my goal.

I didn't want to mess with those 2.5-pound increments again; I wanted to lift 200 pounds or forget about it. So I made sure I was getting enough rest, and on a day when I felt strong,

I warmed up a little, loaded up the bar, took that important breath, and bench pressed 200 pounds for the first time in my life! And I didn't do it as a teenager but as a thirty-five-year-old man!

I won't forget that day. It was June 13, 2013. For seventeen years that goal had haunted me deep down in my mind. The experience of bench pressing 200 pounds really showed me that hard work, focus, and determination, regardless of our age, can go a long way toward helping any one of us reach a goal.

It took me a lot of years to push that extra 2.5 pounds. But I did it!

WHO I AM

It was You who created my inward parts;
You knit me together in my mother's womb.

PSALM 139:13

Most people know me by way of my music and concerts. So there's always this question: "But what about the *real* Josh Turner?" I'd like to think there's little difference between who is on stage and who is at home. If I had to describe myself, this is what I would say:

JOSH TURNER IS . . .

- a man of conviction
- imperfect—but he doesn't let that keep him down
- always striving
- self-disciplined
- a man who loves to laugh
- a man who loves being outdoors
- short-tempered
- kindhearted toward most everybody and everything, but does have a low tolerance for certain things

- creative
- using the God-given gift of his voice
- active, not a couch potato
- a deep thinker—what some would call "an old soul"
- mature beyond his years
- young at heart
- a pretty good judge of character, for the most part
- serious about his roots
- serious about country music—past, present, and future

It's taken me some time to know who I really am. If you haven't already done so, sit back and ask yourself, "Who am I? Really?"

THIS LAND IS OUR LAND

I urge that petitions, prayers, intercessions, and thanksgivings be made for everyone, for kings and all those who are in authority, so that we may lead a tranquil and quiet life in all godliness and dignity. This is good, and it pleases God our Savior, who wants everyone to be saved and to come to the knowledge of the truth.

1 TIMOTHY 2:1–4

I believe we live in a great country. For one, after having traveled across it many times, I can say it's a beautiful country. We have a lot of different freedoms that allow us to live our lives in the way we choose. It's a democracy, so the people have a voice.

If you watch the news every day, though, it's easy to feel like there's nothing but bad going on all the time. And while technology has advanced us as a country, it also gives us instant access to trouble and tragedy, and just the thought of the consequences can feel overwhelming. So it's good to remember that this country is full of honest, hard-working, creative, and talented people who want to see our land not just survive, but thrive.

In 1 Timothy 2 God calls us to pray for our leaders. So I pray for our President and his family and our elected officials, that they would seek God's wisdom, and that God would lead them as they lead our nation. I also pray for the men and women serving in the military—for all of the husbands and wives and sons and daughters who are in harm's way.

I also think it's important to take every opportunity that comes my way to provide entertainment for our troops. On the Fourth of July, 2012, I had the privilege of performing "The Star-Spangled Banner" with the National Symphony Orchestra and my song "Firecracker" on the West Lawn of the Capitol in Washington, DC. I got the chance to meet many members of Congress as well as have the honor of visiting with a lot of the soldiers from Walter Reed Medical Center and their families. I've always had an appreciation for the sacrifice our soldiers make for our country, but my experience that day raised my appreciation to an even higher level. So the very least I can do is to use the talent God has given me to try to put a smile on our soldiers' faces.

Jennifer and I also try to take our boys to as many of the historical landmarks as we can, places like Mount Vernon and Mount Rushmore and Independence Hall. We want our boys to experience these places, not just in a textbook, but in real life. We want them to have a feel for how great our nation

The family and me visiting the Statue of Liberty, New York City, NY

is and their place in it. We want them to grow up to be citizens who abide by the laws of the land and find freedom in that obedience. We also want them to fight for our country in whatever capacity God wants them to. Jennifer and I want our three boys to love their families, work hard, and make sacrifices to help others. That kind of citizen makes America "one nation under God, indivisible, with liberty and justice for all."

MEANS SOMETHING TO ME

Everyone should look out not only for his own
interests, but also for the interests of others.

PHILIPPIANS 2:4

Union Baptist Church in Hannah, South Carolina, has been
talking about building a "life center" that would include a
basketball court, a stage, classrooms, a kitchen, and even day-
care facilities. To some this plan might not mean much, but it
means something to me.

Union Baptist is a very old church. I've got ancestors
who went there, and it was a source of encouragement and of
learning about God's Word in my early life. My parents were
married there, Mamama was choir director for close to forty
years, and I was baptized there. That church was the first place
I ever sang in front of a crowd, both gospel and country. I grew
up in the youth choir, then sang in the adult choir, and finally
became part of a gospel quartet. I was there on Sunday mornings, Sunday evenings, during revivals, and always at summer
Vacation Bible School.

My favorite service was Sunday evening. I meditated a lot

during that time, thinking about what I was going to do with my life. There were never as many people in attendance on Sunday evenings, so the atmosphere was very calm. It was a worshipful time for me and really prepared me for the week ahead.

That "life center" building may come quick, or the project may drag on for years. Who knows? But I plan to contribute financially and help them build it. The deeper truth here is that Union Baptist Church has been a life center for a long, long time. There may not have been a basketball court on-site, but there was room in that church and among those people for this boy to grow and learn and sing and become who I am today. And that means something to me.

COUNTRY—AND PROUD OF IT!

There are doubtless many different kinds of
languages in the world, and all have meaning.

1 CORINTHIANS 14:10

Not only did I grow up in the South, but I grew up out in the country in the South. That fact says a lot about the way I grew up and the way I am and how I've carried myself throughout my life. I was raised on Jerry Clower and Ray Stevens and read articles by Lewis Grizzard and Charlie Walker that were in the *Florence Morning News*. My family has lived a country lifestyle since before cell phones and the Internet and satellite television. As I look back now, it was a refreshing time.

We had our own way of talking as well, our own language. For example, we never said *lunch*. We were only aware of that word because of the lunchroom and lunch ladies and lunchboxes at school. But outside of school, we always referred to lunch as *dinner*, as in *breakfast*, *dinner*, and *supper*.

Then there was the word *kids*. We never said that either. Mamama taught school for years, so we rode with her when we went to middle school. I remember one day her telling me I never needed to use the word *kids* because that's what you call baby goats. The correct word is *children*. I guess she was very persuasive in that moment because I've held on to that and swore I would never say *kids*. And I never have.

When I moved away from home, I began to hear people say *Mom* and *Dad*. But I'd never heard those words where I grew up. We called them *Mama* and *Daddy* and never thought twice about it. But it's rare for me to hear anyone today refer to their parents the way I do.

We even had our clean country cusswords like *I swigger* and *dad-blamed* and *dad-gummit*. We would call certain things or certain people a *scudder*, and when somebody got to smiling real big, my family would say they were *grinnin' like a Chessie* (Cheshire) *cat*. And everybody had nicknames, from family members to everyone in the community. Some were Dummy, Fatty, and Jube (which is short for Jubilation T. Cornpone, the only general who never won a battle). Then there was Coon, Boogie, Stumpy, Drusilla, Buck, Frank Frank, Crow, Sissy, and Doody. And that's just to name a few! In fact, there are some people I grew up with, and I *still* don't know their real names. That was our culture—fun, endearing, and personal. It was a culture unique to the rural South and I've clung to it. Actually, it is part of who I am.

I often refer to Dr. Ralph Stanley, who grew up learning

to speak proper English but chose not to because, where he came from, it wasn't how the people talked. I can totally relate to that. I feel like if I compromise my language and my culture, then I would lose a part of who I am. I'm not willing to do that, certainly not for the sake of trends or political correctness. And hanging on is worth the effort and the strange looks because, at the end of the day, I'll know I've been Josh. I've been me.

BUCKET LIST

Now to Him who is able to do above and beyond all that we ask or
think according to the power that works in us.

EPHESIANS 3:20

Not everyone may call it a "bucket list," but I believe we all have one. And even though we may not be able to accomplish all that's on our list, every single one of us dreams of doing certain things before we die.

I'd love to do some world traveling. I want to see the pyramids in Egypt and the outback of Australia and the Great Wall of China. I would really like to see the Taj Mahal and Stonehenge. I'd like to go on an African safari. I'd even like to visit Antarctica and see the penguins.

I'd love to go on a moose hunt up in Canada for the chance, just once, to shoot at an Alaskan-Yukon moose.

Last but certainly not least, I'd love to earn an induction into the Country Music Hall of Fame. And I'd love for that to happen before I die so I'd have the opportunity to enjoy it a little.

What's on your bucket list? You just never know what God might do to help you check something off!

IF . . .

"Seek first the kingdom of God and His righteousness,
and all these things will be provided for you."

JESUS IN MATTHEW 6:33

If tomorrow I found out that I had only one more week to sing country music, I'd go immediately into the studio and record all the songs I've written—and even some I didn't write. I would do this for posterity, so there would be a final record for future generations, so to speak.

After that, I'd probably move back to South Carolina, back to where I grew up, where my roots are. I imagine I'd try to get a job farming or doing something that involved being outdoors, maybe the Game and Fish Commission or something like that. My job would need to be outside.

Regardless of what I ended up doing, I would continue to do what I'm doing now, which is "seeking first" God's kingdom. God always has a plan. Even if I find myself thinking that everything has fallen through or fallen apart. A verse in the Bible says this: "A man's heart plans his way, but the Lord determines his steps" (Proverbs 16:9). So if I knew I only had a certain amount of time to do something important to me, I hope that I would meditate on that verse to guide my steps!

"A MAN'S HEART PLANS HIS WAY, BUT THE LORD DETERMINES HIS STEPS" (PROVERBS 16:9).

GOOD MEDICINE

A joyful heart is good medicine.

I had always wanted a wooden Indian statue, the kind old cigar shops used to have. I'd been on the lookout for years but had never found the one I wanted. In the summer of '09 I was touring out West, performing some shows, and my daddy was traveling with me. Jennifer was back home, pregnant with Colby, so Daddy kept me company. It was pretty cool getting to spend time with him one-on-one, seeing the country together, just the two of us.

Well, when we were in Wyoming, we decided to take a few days off to see the Tetons and Yellowstone National Park. One day, as we were coming back from Yellowstone, we passed a store that was going out of business. And lined up all across the entrance to the store were wooden Indians. There were about a dozen or so, all about the same height as me. I stopped immediately because the craftsmanship caught my eye. It looked like one of those Indians just might be the statue I'd been looking for! I hurried over to pick out the one I wanted, I paid for it, and the owner of the store wrapped it in a couple of bed sheets and secured them with duct tape. When Daddy and I got back to the tour bus, we found that the only place the statue would fit was in the bottom bunk on the passenger side. So we put it in the bunk and drove on. It looked just like a mummy was laying there.

You can see me? Jackson Hole, WY

The next day I did a show in Montana, then we went on up into western Canada. As we got to the border late that night, the border patrol stopped us and came on the bus to check things out. They drew their flashlights and looked around, opening cabinets and doors. Finally one of the agents came to that bottom bunk and jumped back when he saw the mummy figure.

"Sir, what do you have in this bunk?"

I said, "Oh, just an Indian I got in Wyoming."

He looked really puzzled and said, "I'm going to have to take a look at this, and you're going to have to help me."

I agreed and cut back the bed sheet to reveal a wooden figure. Needless to say, he was very relieved not to find a *real* Indian but a wooden one! We all laughed, and I think he breathed a little easier.

I'm just glad *he* thought it was funny and let us cross the border!

BEING NORMAL AND FAMOUS

Better to be lowly of spirit with the humble
than to divide plunder with the proud.

PROVERBS 16:19

The one thing that never feels normal about my life is being famous. Being recognized while out in public can still catch me off guard after all these years, although I knew recognition came with the job, so to speak.

I have met so many wonderful people because of music, and I sincerely appreciate the fans who approach me and tell me how much my music or a certain song has meant to them. Their support means a great deal, and I never want to take their kind words for granted.

I also have the privilege of joining with other artists and organizations, such as the Make-a-Wish Foundation, that connect me with fans who might not otherwise get to see a show. My desire is to give some hope or comfort as well as pleasure and enjoyment through music. They say the "gift" is supposed to be for the recipient, but I often feel as though I'm the one who is on the receiving end.

I've been blessed in a variety of ways both personally and professionally, and I don't deserve any of it. I am fortunate to make my living by living my dream. I just consider myself an ordinary guy with an extraordinary platform.

Look at who my buddy Devin and I ran into at breakfast . . . the legendary George Jones! I met the Harris family through Make-A-Wish Foundation. Devin Harris was a remarkable young man who made people laugh and smile. I am grateful to have known him.

PAYING ATTENTION

My son, pay attention to my wisdom;
listen closely to my understanding.

PROVERBS 5:1

I read Elizabeth Gilbert's *The Last American Man*, the fascinating true story of American naturalist and one of the History Channel's *Mountain Men*, Eustace Conway. There was a part in the book that told of his time spent with some of the young people of the world. His conclusion was that the biggest downfall of today's youth is the failure to pay attention.

I've noticed that this failure to pay attention is inherent in my boys. They didn't pick this up from somewhere or someone! At times, their failure to pay attention is frustrating, but I've realized that I have to *teach* them the importance of paying attention. I'm always reminding them that their failure to pay attention will get them in trouble, it will get them hurt, or it will hurt someone else. The best thing about paying attention is that you learn so much more about what's going on around you, about life and love and everything in between. And when you learn to pay attention to the simple things in life, you get one step closer to paying attention to God's will for you. And that's when paying attention really pays off!

WHEN YOU LEARN
TO PAY ATTENTION
TO THE SIMPLE
THINGS IN LIFE,
YOU GET ONE
STEP CLOSER TO
PAYING ATTENTION
TO GOD'S WILL
FOR YOU.

HEAVEN

Based on [God's] promise, we wait for the new heavens and a new earth, where righteousness will dwell.

2 PETER 3:13

One of my very favorite books is *90 Minutes in Heaven* by Don Piper. When I first got a copy, I read it in a day. The book is the author's real-life account of spending an hour and a half in heaven after a semitruck crushed his car and he died. One of the first and most dramatic things Don noticed in heaven was the music. He said there was beautiful singing unlike anything he had ever heard on earth. I like that description.

The Bible talks of a new heaven and a new earth. I don't believe heaven will be the stereotypical angels playing harps while reclining on clouds while the rest of us walk around in white robes. No, I think heaven will be a world similar to the one we are living in now, but it will be, as the old preacher said, "the land of no mores"—no more pain, no more suffering, no more futility. Heaven will be full of love and goodness and truth, everything that God is and is about.

I believe that's something definitely worth looking forward to. It'll be like what Adam and Eve had before they gave in to Satan's temptation and sinned. Eden was a beautiful place of beginnings, and I believe heaven will be an equally beautiful place of new beginnings for those who have placed their faith and trust in Jesus Christ.

AT THE MOVIES

Whatever is true, whatever is honorable, whatever is just,
whatever is pure, whatever is lovely, whatever is commendable—if
there is any moral excellence and if there is any praise—
dwell on these things.

PHILIPPIANS 4:8

I love movies and, in particular, action movies. Here are a few of my recommendations:

Rocky Balboa: I love the entire *Rocky* series, and I felt the last installment was a great way to end a great story. It really showcases how someone older can still have dreams and not be afraid to chase them. The movie also shows a father teaching his son about real strength, genuine courage, and how to stand up for what's right even in the face of ridicule.

Open Range: This movie stars two of my favorite actors— Robert Duvall and Kevin Costner. Annette Bening does a wonderful job as well. There are not many current western movies today, and this one is a pleasure to watch. One of the main lessons in this movie was fighting for what's right even if you don't know exactly how to go about it.

A Perfect World: Another Costner film. Contrary to what the title suggests, the movie shows a far-from-perfect world, but Costner's character does become a father figure to a young boy. The message is strong: *a* father figure is better than *no* father figure at all.

Cinderella Man: Russell Crowe portrays James J. Braddock, a boxer who fell on hard times but provided for his family by any means possible. It's a very heartwarming and emotional movie, again focusing on the important role of a father.

The New World: This is Terrence Malick's film about the founding of the Jamestown, Virginia, settlement. Like many of Malick's films, there is not much dialogue, but the visual elements are outstanding. The movie deals with the difference between love that's true and love that's fleeting, fleeing oppression for freedom, and embracing other cultures like Pocahontas was forced to do.

Last but not least would be *The Princess Bride*: While not necessarily an action movie, it stirs up memories of when I watched it as a child. I quote lines from the movie all the time. It's a classic, and anytime I need to laugh, this is the one I go to.

SUCH THINGS

Every generous act and every perfect gift is from above,
coming down from the Father of lights.

JAMES 1:17

In my music and interviews, I really try to talk about the good childhood I had. I try to talk about where I came from, my upbringing, and my faith—and I use personal keepsakes to help me tell my story. Jennifer thinks I'm a hoarder because I keep so much stuff. But I'm one who believes that *stuff* matters: it's evidence of the good, and I cherish it all. As Phil Robertson says, "Score one for the hoarders."

I draw inspiration from the stuff of my life—guns, guitars, books, records, pictures, etc. My music and songs come from the good memories my stuff triggers and the life lessons I've learned along the way from family and friends and God. All that stuff is at the heart of my music, the source from which creativity flows.

I recall that instead of passing all his stuff down to his children, Johnny Cash gave it to an auction company, and they auctioned it off to museums and whoever was willing to pay for it. That was wise: there are a lot of stories of broken sibling relationships because somebody didn't get the stuff they'd wanted for years once their parents died.

I'm gonna have to think that one through, because I've got a lot of stuff!

ROOTS

Then the Lord said to him, "Go back to the land of your fathers
and to your family, and I will be with you."

GENESIS 31:3

I've realized that my boys aren't growing up in the same kinda
world I did. A lot of things have changed since I was a boy.
We live a life of hustle and bustle and busyness. So we try to get
away and spend time at our cabin. It's a place we restored and
made our own. It sits right behind where I grew up in Hannah,
South Carolina.

I think it's valuable for me to go there to remember my
roots. There are dirt roads and farms and struggling families—
it's the world I grew up in. I also think it's good for my boys to
be around people who place value in the simple things and in
each other more than in what they drive or what they wear.

We go to the cabin to get away. But we also go to the cabin
to remember—to remember where we came from. Doing this
helps us decide things like where to go in the future and who
we want to be as a family as well as individually. Most of all,
remembering where we came from reminds us of what love
looks like.

REAL

How painful honest words can be!

JOB 6:25

Just what is *real* country music?

Some people might think that's a complex question, and maybe for some people it is, but not for me. I believe the answer is very straightforward. Plain and simple, real country music is honest songs about real life, love, and heartache.

My radio is set to the XM station Prime Country Channel, which plays all the country hits from the '80s and '90s. Listening to that station will give you a good understanding of what real country music is. Storytelling and raw honesty are the hallmarks of those songs. Whether you're a doctor or a fashion model or a schoolteacher, when you listen to those songs, you can relate because there is a timeless quality to the honesty of the lyrics. The specifics of the song may not fit your life exactly, but the heart of the song rings true: you know deep down what it's talking about.

There's a well-known quote by Hank Williams: "If you can't write a song in twenty minutes, then it ain't worth writing." Now, granted, that's up for discussion, but his point is valid. If you can't sit down and write about a real-life situation in a short amount of time, then the song probably won't be real, honest, and natural. It will be contrived, and people recognize that every time. There *have* been exceptions to this rule, but very few.

People know *real* when they hear it. This is also true about faith. Most people can tell when someone is a religious phony only out for themselves. Being real in your faith is a surefire way to help those in need and make this world a better place. That's something I wish we all would strive for.

HOW MUCH LAND DOES A MAN NEED?

Don't neglect to do what is good and to share,
for God is pleased with such sacrifices.

HEBREWS 13:16

A word that runs deep in my family is *legacy*. Because of this I have a great interest in knowing who and where I came from. I believe that's one way you find out who you are.

My great-great-great-granddaddy was James D. Turner. He was an ancestor of mine nobody ever told me about. I found out about him after doing some genealogical research. I also found out he's buried less than a mile from my house!

Well, James D. Turner owned a lot of land, and at some point he donated half an acre to the Bethlehem Methodist Episcopal Church, which in those days (the early 1800s) was a huge gift! As you might imagine, over time the church has moved from its original location. The name has slightly changed to Bethlehem United Methodist Church, but family members of that original church are still gathering together. So part of their spiritual heritage can be traced all the way back to the sacrifice my great-great-great-granddaddy made.

Because of his spirit of giving, his legacy lives on, and people continue to worship God.

The sacrificial giving of one of my ancestors is both an example and a challenge to me. My desire is to leave a legacy as well, different in kind but similar in spirit. For with such sacrifices God is pleased.

PAPA TURNER

Do not be hasty to speak, and do not be impulsive
to make a speech before God. God is in heaven and
you are on earth, so let your words be few.

ECCLESIASTES 5:2

P apa Turner was my granddaddy and the epitome of a man of few words.

Papa's full name was Drexell Turner; he didn't have a middle name. He was born in 1920 and died at the age of 80 in 2001. He was probably one of the hardest working men, and certainly one of the strongest men for his size, I've ever known. He loved his wife and children, was very active in church, and never had anything bad to say about anybody. What words he did use were always good.

For most of my life, I remember Papa Turner working in a factory in Johnsonville, South Carolina. But before I came along, he served in Germany during World War II. He didn't talk much about that. I had to learn on my own that he drove an ambulance and was shot and injured one night while out on a run. He was awarded the Purple Heart for his service. He never talked about that either.

Papa Turner (seated) in Germany during World War II

One thing I remember clearly about Papa Turner was that he kept his belongings very clean and very organized. He and Granny didn't really have a lot of money or stuff, so what they did have, they took a lot of pride in and took good care of. That was a huge lesson I learned from them, one I try to teach my boys: it doesn't matter if you have a lot or a little; it's important to appreciate what you have, take pride in it, and take care of it.

When Papa Turner finally retired, he got to do what he loved most, and that was to work in his garden. He had one of the most impeccable gardens you would ever see. He grew everything he could—from collard greens to watermelons to corn to okra to sweet potatoes. In fact, I remember seeing an eight-pound sweet potato from his garden. That's right! Eight pounds!

Papa Turner told all of his children that he wanted them to do better financially than he had in life. He didn't want them to have to struggle as much as he had. Well, after graduating high school and marrying Mama, Daddy wanted to go to college, so he asked Papa Turner for help. He said he couldn't help Daddy financially, but Papa Turner did encourage him to go to college anyway and to do well.

So Daddy and Mama alternated between work and school. Daddy worked while Mama went to school, and then they flip-flopped: Mama worked while Daddy went to school.

With Papa Turner's constant encouragement, they each graduated.

The day Papa Turner died, he was out in the garden working a tiller. He stopped to take a break and cool off from the heat. He went and sat down in a folding chair under a shade tree near the garden. And that's where he was found, upright and looking peaceful.

Papa Turner was a man of few words, but he made up for it by being a man of great dedication and great love.

Papa Turner's 8 lb. sweet potato. The scale doesn't lie!

CHASING MY DREAMS

Your old men will have dreams,
and your young men will see visions.

JOEL 2:28

Where I grew up, most men followed in their daddy's footsteps when they chose how to make a living. So I was not surrounded by a lot of dreamers; most young men I knew settled for their father's dreams. My daddy was different. He *did* have dreams, but he never got to do what he really wanted to do—and that was to be an engineer. He was a hard worker and had a bright mind, but he found out he was color-blind, and because of that, his dream got squashed.

Daddy ended up working for Farm Bureau Insurance Company. He was an agent for nineteen years. It's all I've ever seen him do. I never learned about the insurance business because he didn't feel compelled to pass that line of work on to me. I can't tell you how thankful I am for that!

Daddy knew I had a gift for music and singing. Instead of having me follow in his footsteps, he encouraged me to chase my dreams. He knew I wouldn't catch all my dreams, but he wanted to see me fly as high as I could, to pursue them whether they came about or not.

A lot of the guys I grew up with, though, simply were not dreamers. I believe they learned that resignation at home. But that's not how it was in our house. My daddy wanted me to be more than he was, go further than he went, and see more in life than he saw. That is my prayer for my boys too.

FEELING LOW AT A HIGH ALTITUDE

I cry aloud to God,
aloud to God, and He will hear me.
I sought the Lord in my day of trouble.
My hands were continually lifted up
all night long;
I refused to be comforted.
I think of God; I groan;
I meditate; my spirit becomes weak. *Selah*
You have kept me from closing my eyes;
I am troubled and cannot speak.
I consider days of old,
years long past.
At night I remember my music;
I meditate in my heart, and my spirit ponders.
"Will the Lord reject forever
and never again show favor?
Has His faithful love ceased forever?
Is His promise at an end for all generations?
Has God forgotten to be gracious?
Has He in anger withheld His compassion?" *Selah*
So I say, "I am grieved

that the right hand of the Most High has changed."
I will remember the LORD's works;
yes, I will remember Your ancient wonders.
I will reflect on all You have done
and meditate on Your actions.

PSALM 77:1–12

I know what the psalmist is talking about. I really do. . . .

I have a friend who lives in Colorado. A couple of years ago he invited me out for an elk hunt. I was very excited about the trip, and my tags and all my gear were ready to go. But a few days before leaving I came down with a head cold. I thought I'd probably get over it by the time I got to Colorado, but as I drove to the airport, I remember thinking that maybe I should cancel the trip and reschedule. I just didn't feel good, and I couldn't say that I was getting any better.

As my plane landed in Denver, my left ear completely stopped up. I was miserable; I could hardly hear anything or anyone. But I kept going. As I drove the rental car over Vail Pass, my ear opened up, and I thought that maybe I could do this hunt after all. But as I drove down the pass, my ear closed back up again. That initial excitement of being on an elk hunt had faded fast.

I met my friend and we hunted that evening but didn't see anything. We got up at 3 a.m. the next morning and headed out to a cabin that belonged to a friend of his, a cabin that ended up being as far away from civilization as I've ever been. Later that morning the hunt began, and things went from bad to worse. As we hiked up and down at over 9,000 feet, I went from sweating profusely, to having chills, to shivering all over. I was having a hard time breathing, and my legs were scream-ing at me to stop. I was completely miserable. We did see a few elk, but they were too far away to get a good shot. When we got back to the cabin, I literally thought I was going to die. I called my doctor, and he thought I might have high-altitude sickness, which affects a lot of people, but without examining me, he wasn't certain.

To make a long story a little shorter, we finally got back to town, and my buddy took me to a doctor friend of his. The doctor checked me out and diagnosed me with bronchitis, something I'd never had. He gave me an antibiotic that got me through the next couple of days, but we never saw any more elk. I thought the whole trip was a bust.

But that's the deal with hunting. Sometimes you're sick and miserable, and you don't see any elk, and you wish you'd just stayed home. And sometimes you feel great, and the weather is perfect, and you get to take the shot you'd dreamed about. Without the bust times, the boom times wouldn't mean as much—and neither would have the same meaning without experiencing both. The main thing to remember in the bust times is this: just because things didn't turn out the way you thought they would doesn't mean God has forsaken you. He's still there with you and for you. That's when it's important to do like the psalmist did and "reflect on all [God] has done" to get you through.

It can only go up from there.

BE YOURSELF

Make yourself an example of good works with
integrity and dignity in your teaching.

TITUS 2:7

I've got a lot of friends who don't share my faith. And that's okay. I don't shy away from those kinds of friends. I've learned a lot from them, and I always look at our friendship as a chance for me to be a light just by being myself. It feels natural to me.

I've never considered myself the missionary type, but I've always been grounded in my faith. My parents have called it *stubborn*; I call it *convicted*. I want people to see that I've got a strong faith as well as a sharp sense of humor, that I love to have fun and be happy. I believe that by way of my music and lifestyle, I can have a big impact on other people. Again, not in some forced way, but naturally. I want my life to be contagious, infectious to the point of people asking, "What's different about you, Josh?"

One person who did just that was my very first vocal coach. I ended up leading her to the Lord. At the time she was helping me rehabilitate from a serious voice injury. And even though I didn't know it, I was helping her by just being me, by being very open and honest, talking like I normally talk about things I normally talk about. She started asking me questions about my faith, and before long she decided to become a Christian. Then she and her husband started going to church. The end result was that their lives were completely changed. That really surprised me because it happened just by me being me. That's the only person God needs me to be—*me*.

GOOD COMPANY

How happy is the man
who does not follow the advice of the wicked
or take the path of sinners
or join a group of mockers!

PSALM 1:1

He was my granddaddy and my mama's daddy. We called him Papa Weaver, and he had an awesome sense of humor. I loved listening to him. When he would talk about the people you should surround yourself with, the company you oughta keep, he'd say, "If you hang around a cow pasture long enough, you're bound to step in . . ." Well, I think you can probably finish his thought—and it's a pretty good lesson for life. I've never forgotten that.

I've had to teach my oldest boy this lesson. While I haven't used Papa Weaver's exact words, I do believe I've captured the heart of it: "It's okay to go against the grain." I've tried to impress on Hampton that there'll be children in school, on the baseball team, even at church, who will be involved in things that aren't good for them, not to mention him. I've told

Papa Weaver and Mamama

him he can follow them, but that kind of company guarantees he's gonna get in trouble like them. And if he's not real careful, *he* might be the one getting in trouble instead of them.

I don't know if it ever gets easier to go against the grain as you get older, but it's sure not easy when you're young. I think Papa Weaver knew that, maybe even from his own experience. I didn't always listen well, but I did listen. That's my hope for my sons too, that they'll keep listening to my rendition of my granddaddy's advice: "It's okay to go against the grain."

PRIORITIES

The precepts of the LORD are right,
making the heart glad;
the command of the LORD is radiant,
making the eyes light up.

PSALM 19:8

Every morning it feels the same: there's so much to be done, it's overwhelming. Some people talk about the ten thousand things they have to do; for us, it's more like the ten

Jennifer and me, Laguna Beach, CA

million things. So Jennifer and I have to constantly stop and remind ourselves to prioritize, to stay focused on what really matters to us, and then to accept that what doesn't get done that day will likely still be there for the next.

The other day we were all home together, all five of us. We enjoyed some pizza that Jennifer had made, and when we finished, we walked behind the shop where I showed her the cross Hampton and I had made for Moses' gravesite. Jennifer didn't seem to like it very much. So I prioritized and took the five-gallon bucket half full of water that I was holding and dowsed her with it. That started a water war, and the boys loved it!

There were plenty of other things we could have been doing that day—things that were on that never-ending list. But setting that list aside and having a little play was the most important thing to do in that moment, for our boys as well as for Jennifer and me. And the laughter we shared was worth every drop.

A PLACE OF REST

"Come to Me, all of you who are weary and burdened, and I will give you rest. All of you, take up My yoke and learn from Me, because I am gentle and humble in heart, and you will find rest for yourselves. For My yoke is easy and My burden is light."

JESUS IN MATTHEW 11:28–30

I've mentioned our cabin in South Carolina earlier in the book as being an important place for my family to reconnect. It's also an important place for me when I need time alone. My lifestyle is so fast paced and complex. I wear many different hats all at the same time. If I'm not careful, I'll try to control and micromanage everything—essentially getting in God's way instead of letting Him lead me in the direction He wants me to go. I don't want that to be the case, so to keep that from happening, I go to the cabin to get away from it all and focus on Him.

I've found, though, that whenever I get to the cabin, the first day or so I actually have a lonesome feeling. I find the peace and quiet and slowness of it all intimidating. I have to work at turning off all the activity in my head. But after a few days pass, I start decompressing and de-stressing, and the things that are most important in my life begin to come back into focus. I start feeling better emotionally, physically, and mentally. I start finding joy in the simplest things.

Being at the cabin gives me time to think. There's no television or phone, so I'm not distracted by noise or interruptions. Whether I'm outside working or walking in the woods or fishing on the river, I've got the freedom to think and pray and listen. I have the opportunity to open up my heart and mind and spirit to what God wants to say to me. Being in that simple place surrounded by God's artistry allows me to step back and realize that God is in control, not me, and that His yoke is easy and His burden is light. Taking time away to remember this truth allows me then to go back to Nashville and take wise steps toward my future and the future of my family. Taking time away allows me to find rest for myself—something God promises I'll have if I'll just stop and pay attention to Him.

THE WAY IT IS

Let us run with endurance the race that lies before us, keeping our eyes on Jesus, the source and perfecter of our faith, who for the joy that lay before Him endured a cross and despised the shame and has sat down at the right hand of God's throne.

HEBREWS 12:1–2

My daddy wasn't what you would call a motivational speaker. There were never any lights and cameras, and he didn't give ten-minute speeches. He was very direct and concise when it came to giving life lessons. One of the main lessons I learned from him was presented to me in one sentence: "Sometimes you're gonna have to do things you don't want to do."

I imagine that's the way it was when Jesus prayed in the garden and asked His Father if there was any way He might avoid the cross. The answer He received, in my words, was "No, this will be hard. But there's goodness ahead if You'll just endure." And so, as the verse in Hebrews 12 says, Jesus did the hard work He didn't necessarily want to do, but He did it anyway. He trusted His heavenly Father, just like I've trusted Daddy, and just how I hope my boys will learn to trust me: "Sometimes you're gonna have to do things you don't want to do." That's just the way it is.

MEN AND CHURCH

Let us be concerned about one another in order to promote love and good works, not staying away from our worship meetings, as some habitually do, but encouraging each other, and all the more as you see the day drawing near.

HEBREWS 10:24–25

Some people have asked me my thoughts as to why men don't go to church. That's a little strange for me to think about because where I grew up, the men *did* go to church. There were only a few I knew of who didn't, but even then, those men would show up on holidays or for special occasions. I always wondered about those men and how their absence from church affected their families. . . . Anyway, I don't know that there's any one specific reason why some men have an aversion to church. But here are a few of my thoughts.

Going to church requires something of you, and some of those requirements are things some men don't care for. For example, listening. Men can tend to be poor listeners. A church service involves sitting still and listening. Some men would rather be active, doing something. The thought of sitting still for an hour or so works about as well for some men as it does for most boys. In other words, it doesn't.

There's also the requirement of getting dressed for the service, what people used to refer to as "putting on your Sunday best." I don't think church should be a fashion show by any means, but I do believe that getting dressed up, if for just one day during the week, is good for you.

One more thing. Church is also a kind of social atmosphere that some men shy away from, especially if there's much of a crowd.

Beyond those three factors are, in my opinion, two biggies. First of all, shame. Some men feel like they don't measure up to the church crowd and that they'd be judged if they showed up for a service. Church should be the last place anyone should feel judged, but I know judgment happens. Instead of experiencing church as a welcoming place, some men have felt the exact opposite.

Then there's pride. Some men feel like they have life all figured out, and they don't have any character flaws or blemishes—so why would they need a church service or a sermon or a prayer time? There's very little that can break through to a man lost in his pride except pain. And sometimes that's the only way to get him in church.

Church is not a perfect place. How could it be? It's full of imperfect people who make mistakes and have problems. It's a place full of people who are hurting and struggling just to find their way. But the whole point of the church is to learn about the Lord and His Word, His truth, His love, and His grace. It's a place to find forgiveness for our faults and to improve our lives. I encourage anyone not to shy away from church.

I'm glad I grew up where the men went to church. They were leaders there, in the community, and in their homes and they were a great example to young boys like me. I'm trying to be that same kind of example for my boys.

LONG ENOUGH

"Whoever is faithful in very little is also faithful in much."

JESUS IN LUKE 16:10

Some people leave our lives much too quickly. At least that's what I think. But I've found that if we look back closely, we realize they were around exactly long enough. That's how it was with Granny.

Her name was Dora, and she was my daddy's mama. She was the mother of six children, one of which had Down's syndrome. She never got past a fourth-grade education, so she never got a driver's license, therefore she never drove a car. So she stayed in the house and made it a home.
I remember Granny as some-
one always singing, always
laughing, and just a joy to be
around. She never took her-
self too seriously. It's not that
she was silly, but lighthearted.
I guess that's the best way to
live: try to make things light.

Granny and me at her house, Hannah, SC

Granny was diagnosed with breast cancer in 1977. She knew that I was about to be born, so she prayed, "Lord, I just want to live long enough to see this child." Well, I was born on November 20 that same year. And as God would have it, Granny lived until the day before my tenth birthday, and the love and wisdom she poured into my life for almost ten years is priceless. Her impact on me was very profound.

If it were up to me, I'd have had Granny live longer, a lot longer. But such matters aren't up to me. Life and death are in God's hands. And while I still feel she left too quickly, I can clearly see she was here for as long as God needed her to be. So I'll choose to let that be long enough for me.

FELLOW WARRIORS

These are the names of David's mighty warriors . . .

2 SAMUEL 23:8 NIV

I was glad when I read that John Eldredge is not a fan of the word *accountability*. "Having an accountability partner" sounds too soft for me, even mushy. I've never felt compelled to call somebody up and see how they were handling their sin or vice versa.

> *We don't need accountability groups;*
> *we need fellow warriors,*
> *someone to fight alongside, someone to watch our back.*
>
> —JOHN ELDREDGE, *Wild at Heart*

Yes! What a man needs is a fellow warrior, not an accountant, and surely not a mother hen. I believe if you're genuinely doing life together, this whole accountability thing starts to look pretty manly. You don't have men who are checking in on you at regularly scheduled times but men who are right alongside you, fighting the battle for faith, family, and friends every day.

The men I've surrounded myself with know me and trust me, just like I know and trust them. They are much more than accountants; they're brothers. I'd bleed for them, and they would for me; it's happened before, and it'll happen again. Life is a battle, and a battle demands warriors.

THIRD TIME'S A CHARM

Take delight in the LORD,
and He will give you your heart's desires.

PSALM 37:4

Earlier in the book I told my elk hunt story that didn't exactly go the way I'd hoped. Well, that BUST time made me really appreciate this BOOM time. . . .

It happened during a recent trip to Colorado, and it was my third attempt at getting a bull elk. I started hunting on Sunday with my buddy Ed, and we hiked off and on from 6:30 a.m. to 5 p.m., all over Coffin Mountain—and that mountain is very aptly named! When we got only about halfway up, I thought I was going to *end up* in a coffin! Ed's house is at about 8000 feet, and the top of Coffin Mountain is over 9200 feet, and both of those altitudes are quite different from the 760 feet of my house in Nashville. Needless to say, I didn't have an easy time adjusting to that thin air.

I don't know if I ever really acclimated to the altitude, but I did have an easier time as we went along. And I was glad about that because Ed and I really hunted hard. We gave everything we had in our effort to find me a bull elk.

When we got almost to the top of the mountain, we were cow calling, when all of a sudden a bull elk bugled back at us. That was the very first time I'd heard a bugle in the wild, and it was absolutely incredible! We hoped the bull elk would come on in, but it never did. So we kept on hiking.

Eventually we hid in a stand of quaking aspens—Ed calls them "quakies"—and started calling again. We heard another bugle, and as we followed the sound, we could actually smell the elk. I had heard that you can sometimes smell the musk of an elk before you even hear their call, so I was pretty excited to experience it for myself. We kept hiking toward the bugle, and when we got into some thick, shaded pine trees, we walked right up on a really young bull elk, but it was too young to shoot. Looking around, though, we saw a lot of signs—a lot more than one young bull would make—so we suspected that other elk had run off. We hiked over to a ridge and called some more, and after a few minutes we heard another cow call, but it never showed its face. But after a few minutes, we heard a shot, so we think we actually spooked some bigger elk toward another hunter.

At that point we decided to go back down around the mountain and head for home and get some much-needed sleep. The next morning we stepped outside to find it had snowed just enough to cover the ground. After talking about our options, we decided to hunt in a different spot, and on our way there, we came across a bull elk track that we followed for miles and miles through very thick brush and some of the roughest country I'd ever been in. By then I felt pushed to my physical limits. On top of that, fog had rolled in, and our visibility wasn't very good. So we headed back to the house for a few hours to rest and wait for the fog to lift. At that point I was starting to have flashbacks from my past hunts—my bust times—and trying not to get discouraged. And I started counting down the days I had left to hunt and knew my time was limited.

That evening we returned to our morning spot. As we walked along, Ed let out a cow call, and about a minute later I saw a tan spot about 300 yards away on the side of the canyon. I asked Ed for his binoculars and focused in. It was definitely an elk—and definitely a big enough elk for me to shoot. Ed said, "Take your time. Get a steady shot."

I propped my elbows up on my knees, aimed, took a deep breath, and fired. I hit that bull elk in the right front shoulder, and it fell right where it had been standing. I ended up with a 4 x 5 (nine-point) elk. It was my BOOM moment, and I was elated! I ended up getting almost 200 pounds of meat and had the head mounted for my cottage.

This hunt was very exciting for me. It was great being out in God's creation with my friend, and it was especially great

My first elk, Eagle, CO

to finally shoot a bull elk. I'd been praying, asking God to give me an elk. And I believe God heard my prayers and answered them, not the first time, not the second time, but the third. Sometimes getting His yes is about persistence, about not giving up.

SOMETIMES GETTING [GOD'S] YES IS ABOUT PERSISTENCE, ABOUT NOT GIVING UP.

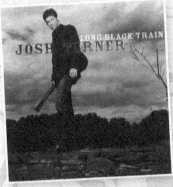

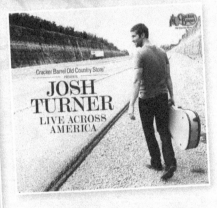

TWITTER: @joshturnermusic

FACEBOOK: facebook.com/joshturner

For more information on The Josh Turner Scholarship Fund go to

www.cfmt.org/giving-and-investing/become-a-donor/give-to-a-fund/josh-turner-scholarship-fund/.